Liberal Education and the Democratic Ideal

and other essays

New enlarged edition

A. Whitney Griswold

President of Yale University

Liberal Education and

the Democratic Ideal

AND OTHER ESSAYS

New Haven and London

Yale University Press

Introduction

Whoever touches upon the subject of liberal education strikes a chord with many echoes. In fact, more often than not, what he strikes is not a chord but a discord. There is little harmony among American educators with respect to this particular type of education. Many consider it a thing of the past and regard those who still argue its merits as reactionaries, while in the opposite direction equally disdainful views of its detractors are entertained. My purpose is neither to augment the discord nor, necessarily, to diminish it. I do not believe liberal education to be a universal prescription—or panacea—for all American youth. But neither do I believe it to be a thing of the past. I believe it is a thing of the present and the future.

Every writer on such subjects as this likes to think of himself as objective, and most lay claims to this effect. I have striven for objectivity, especially in the use of historical evidence in which I was trained. But I would not have undertaken my task in the first place if I had not believed in my subject.

I came to this belief through the study (and teaching) of history. Up to that point I had been happy in the subjective experience of a liberal education without clearly perceiving or being much interested in its objective value. My study of history convinced me of this value. When Thomas Jefferson called education "the most legitimate engine of government" he stated a general truth which, however, modern dictatorships could (and did) pervert by suborning their educators. When he defined liberal education as the most vital part of that most legitimate engine he stated a particular truth no free society or democratic government can ignore. For, said Jefferson, "If a nation expects to be ignorant and free, in a state of civilization, it expects what never was and never will be." If we test this proposition against the experience of our own lives and times we must conclude, I think, that, while ignorant nations may remain free if uncivilized, and civilized nations may be enslaved if kept ignorant, the surest safeguard against either fate is an education that contributes directly to knowledge, freedom, and civilization.

Such I believe to be the distinctive nature of liberal education. Not only does it concern itself more directly and vitally than any other type of education with the good life that is the end of all political society; it also shows a like concern for the means whereby that society is to be governed and the good life achieved. I believe its fate is bound up with the fate of our political society. Along with the individual freedom we guarantee to our citizens goes the expectation that they will use that freedom to better themselves and thus better society. We look to their individual self-improvement as the only certain means of ensuring the security and welfare of the state. The purpose of liberal education is to expand to the limit the individual's capacity —and desire—for self-improvement, for seeking and finding enjoyment and meaning in everything he does. Thus does liberal education serve the purpose of democracy.

With a few minor changes the essays that follow stand exactly as they were written. The first five discuss the general nature of liberal education, its origin, history, and fundamental purposes. The rest deal in various ways with the environment in which we can expect liberal education to fulfil its aims and perform its historic role. All have been published before. For permission to reprint them here I am indebted to the following, among others: The *New York Times Magazine,* the *Saturday Review, Harper's Magazine,* the *Ladies' Home Journal,* the *New York Herald Tribune,* and the *American Academy of Arts and Letters.* The dates of their original publication range from 1951 to 1958.

A few of my chapters contain topical references which I thought would spoil them to remove yet which might be confusing if unexplained. Chapter Six, *On Reading,* was originally written and delivered as an address on the occasion of the third National Book Awards in 1952. The audience of literary craftsmen accounts for its opening and concluding lines. My reading list has changed since I wrote this chapter, but not my reading habits; and my convictions with respect to the uses and importance of reading have strengthened. Reading is a sadly neglected part of the American educational process, from school through college.

Chapter Fourteen, *Freedom, Security, and the University Tradition* was originally written and delivered at the Bicentennial exercises of Columbia University in 1954. I thought it well to leave its beginning and conclusion unchanged, since they both lend historical substance to the tradition with which it deals.

Chapter Fifteen, *The Cost of Freedom, An Academic View,* was written and delivered as an address to the Association of American Colleges at Philadelphia in 1957, not long after the Hungarian rebellion. It is important to identify this audience in order to make plain my use of the phrase "preaching to the converted." With respect to academic freedom, I am sure I was doing precisely that; with respect to liberal education, I am not so sure. The declining number of college and university students majoring in the liberal arts cited in the address (below, p. 146) was a fact to be conjured with at the time. Meanwhile the invasion of the undergraduate curricula of our liberal arts colleges by vocational and "pre-professional" studies has continued so briskly that in some cases it calls into question the term by which these colleges are known. I was not, therefore, preaching wholly to the converted, or to the wholly converted, and I am all the more grateful to my audience for the courteous hearing they gave me.

One more chapter may benefit by a word of explanation. Chapter Eleven, *Further Obsequies for the Grammarian,* was written and delivered as the Evangeline Wilbour Blashfield Foundation address before the American Academy of Arts and Letters and the National Institute of Arts and Letters in 1958, and is published in their *Proceedings* for that year. I am particularly grateful for their permission to republish it here.

One final editorial comment. The reader will notice that I have laid much emphasis on the responsibility of our secondary schools for liberal education. I have done this not to minimize the responsibility of our colleges and universities or to cover up their shortcomings in discharging it, but rather because liberal education must begin in secondary school if it is to begin at all. If liberal education is to assume its rightful and proportionate place in our educational system, the colleges must do everything in their power to ensure that it is properly begun in the schools and then carry it to fruition in their own curricula. In this they share an indivisible responsibility with the schools.

A. W. G.

New Haven, Connecticut
September 1958

ADDENDA FOR SECOND EDITION

In this edition, six new chapters have been added to those included in the first edition. These are Chapter Eight, *The Fine Arts and the University,* which appeared in the *Atlantic* in 1959; Chapter Nine, *The Best of Two Worlds: Athletics and Education,* from *Sports Illustrated,* 1955; Chapter Ten, *The Alumnus as Patron of Learning,* written in 1962; Chapter Sixteen, *The Colleges and the Loyalty Oath,* from the *New York Times Magazine,* 1959; Chapter Eighteen, *Going to the Devil,* written in 1960; and Chapter Twenty, *An Interview,* which was conducted on the subject of "The University" and published under that title by the Center for the Study of Democratic Institutions in 1961. Permission of the original publishers to reprint this material is gratefully acknowledged.

A. W. G.

Martha's Vineyard
August 1962

Contents

Contents

Liberal Education and
the Democratic Ideal

The ideal of liberal education lies at the very roots of American history. For centuries this type of education had been esteemed throughout western civilization as the education of the ideal citizen. But the political and social structure of that civilization had denied access to such education to all but a privileged few. To uphold an ideal of citizenship and then deny citizens the means of attaining it was difficult to justify in logic and impossible in democratic philosophy. Even if such attainment could not be guaranteed to all citizens, it should at least be the opportunity of all. The educational route to ideal citizenship should be open to all were able to travel it; and all who showed such promise should be encouraged to strike out upon it and proceed as far as native intelligence and industry could carry them.

Such was the educational philosophy of the founders of our country. "The Puritans," John Adams wrote in his *Dissertation on the Canon and Feudal Law* in 1765, "transmitted to their posterity . . . a hereditary ardor for liberty and thirst for knowledge. They were convinced, by their knowledge of human nature, derived from history and their own experience, that nothing could preserve their posterity from the encroachments of the two systems of tyranny, in opposition to which, as has been observed al-

1

ready, they erected their government in church and state, but knowledge diffused generally through the whole body of the people. Their civil and religious principles, therefore, conspired to prompt them to use every measure and take every precaution in their power to propagate and perpetuate knowledge. For this purpose they laid very early the foundations of colleges, and invested them with ample privileges and emoluments; and it is remarkable that they have left among their posterity so universal an affection and veneration for those seminaries, and for liberal education, that the meanest of the people contribute cheerfully to the support and maintenance of them every year, and that nothing is more generally popular than projections for the honor, reputation, and advantage of those seats of learning. But the wisdom and benevolence of our fathers rested not here. They made an early provision by law that every town consisting of so many families should be always furnished with a grammar school. They made it a crime for such a town to be destitute of a grammar schoolmaster for a few months, and subjected it to a heavy penalty. So that the education of all ranks of people was made the care and expense of the public, in a manner that I believe has been unknown to any other people ancient or modern."

"Laws for the liberal education of youth," concluded Adams in his influential *Thoughts on Government* in 1776, "especially of the lower class of people, are so extremely wise and useful, that, to a humane and generous mind, no expense for this purpose would be thought extravagant."

Adams' thoughts on education were shared by Madison, who has been called Father of the Constitution, and by Jefferson, his tutor. All three men, whose combined influence upon the shaping of our government was so great and in whose several works one finds the most comprehensive exposition of the theory and meaning of that government, saw in

2

education not merely the corollary to democracy but the key, the *sine qua non*. In their system of education all three assigned the paramount role to liberal education. What did they mean by the term? One has but to read John Adams' letter recommending his son John Quincy Adams for admission to Harvard, or Jefferson's educational advices to his nephew, Peter Carr, to discover that they meant exactly what we mean by it.

They did not regard it as a panacea to be forced down unwilling throats or consumed by all in equal doses with identical results. They thought of it, and wrote of it, as part of a comprehensive system that began with reading, writing, and arithmetic for all, included vocational training, and progressed through the most advanced phases of higher learning. At each successive stage high standards were to be met, and progressively higher and more exalted labors awaited the survivors. This is how Jefferson described the system in a letter to Adams in 1813:

> At the first session of our legislature after the Declaration of Independence, we passed a law abolishing entails. And this was followed by one abolishing the privilege of primogeniture, and dividing the lands of intestates equally among all their children, or other representatives. These laws, drawn by myself, laid the axe to the foot of pseudo-aristocracy. And had another which I prepared been adopted by the legislature, our work would have been complete. It was a bill for the more general diffusion of learning. This proposed to divide every county into wards of five or six miles square, like your townships; to establish in each ward a free school for reading, writing and common arithmetic; to provide for the annual selection of the best subjects from these schools, who might receive, at the public expense, a higher degree of education at a district

school; and from these district schools to select a certain number of the most promising subjects to be completed at an University, where all the useful sciences should be taught. Worth and genius would thus have been sought out from every condition of life, and completely prepared by education for defeating the competition of wealth and birth for public trusts.

By such means, said Jefferson, in his *Notes on Virginia*, the "best geniuses" would be "raked from the rubbish," and society would be provided with "an education adapted to the years, to the capacity, and the condition of everyone, and directed to their freedom and happiness."

The political context of these educational ideas is particularly significant. A highly selective educational system appears side by side with laws abolishing primogeniture and entail, not as an exception to them, but as their fulfillment. Raking genius from the rubbish was a means of laying the axe to pseudo-aristocracy. The whole system, with its ultimate aims of a general diffusion of knowledge and the freedom and happiness of everyone, revolved around the principle of seeking out "worth and genius . . . from every condition of life" and preparing it "by education . . . for public trusts."

Here was no dogmatic leveling or rationalizing of privilege in the name of "leadership." Worth and genius were just as vital to democracy as to any other type of society. To the extent that power and responsibility are diffused in a democracy, they were more vital. Unless democracy was prepared to renounce their accomplishments—which, of course, it was not—it must find its own way of producing them. Far from stifling or retarding worth and genius, it must devise truly democratic means of discovering them and capitalizing their powers for the benefit of society.

4

Liberal education supplied these means. No one should be denied access to it because of his condition of life. None who gained access should be retarded because of someone else's condition of mentality. There was no distinction between public and private responsibility in this regard. Those who could afford to pay their way through school and university were to do so, those who could not were to be carried at public expense, both being subject to the same educational qualifications. The important thing was the educational process. This was democracy's answer to a universal need, the best answer any nation had given so far, the best and surest any has given to date.

The role of liberal education is defined in the preamble to Jefferson's *Bill for the More General Diffusion of Knowledge* as follows:

> And whereas it is generally true that people will be happiest whose laws are best, and are best administered, and that laws will be wisely formed, and honestly administered, in proportion as those who form and administer them are wise and honest; whence it becomes expedient for promoting the publick happiness that those persons, whom nature hath endowed with genius and virtue, should be rendered by liberal education worthy to receive, and able to guard the sacred deposit of the rights and liberties of their fellow citizens, and that they should be called to that charge without regard to wealth, birth or other accidental condition or circumstance . . .

The bill goes on to provide that the books used to teach children reading and writing in elementary schools should be "such as will at the same time make them acquainted with Graecian, Roman, English, and American history"; and that students in secondary (or as Jefferson called them, grammar) schools should "be taught the Latin and Greek languages, English grammar, geography and the higher part of numerical arithmetick, to wit, vulgar and decimal fractions, and the extraction of the square and cube roots."

It is hardly necessary to cite further evidence of the importance Jefferson attached to liberal education. It was perhaps the principal inspiration of his life. It runs as a major theme through all his works—his public papers and his private correspondence—informing and prompting him at every stage of his career. It is reflected in his omnivorous reading, his love of learning in every field, and the ingenuity and versatility with which he turned it to practical account. "Nothing could be sounder than your view of the importance of laying a broad foundation in other branches of knowledge whereon to raise the superstructure of any particular science which one would chuse to profess with credit and usefulness," he wrote one of his friends in the fullness of his experience, in 1811. Jefferson's life was a monument to that principle. He not only preached liberal education; he personified it.

One could wish for a more general knowledge of these facts in the United States today. There appears to be a disposition to regard high educational standards as undemocratic, and liberal education as either useless or beyond our intellectual competence. It is hard to understand how anyone acquainted with the mind and spirit of the founders of our country could entertain such views. There is no country that owes so much of its very existence to liberal education as the United States.

Liberal Education Is
Practical Education

It is beginning to dawn on the American people, and, I
hope, to trouble their conscience, that all is not well with
their schools. Headline after headline extends the nation-
wide report of overcrowded schoolrooms and teacher shortages. What the headlines do not tell us is how vitally these
conditions are affecting our chances of survival, not just in
the "cold war," but in the historical perspective of Western
civilization.

We have waked up to the necessity for conserving our
natural resources, to the topsoil blowing around the prairies
and floating down the Mississippi. We are still fighting off
sleep in recognizing and attacking the far more serious wastage of our human resources. A little over a hundred years
ago Charles Dickens deplored "the monstrous neglect of education in England, and the disregard of it by the state as a
means of forming good or bad citizens, and miserable or
happy men." We shall have to bestir ourselves to escape the
same censure and prevent the cultural catastrophe that
would follow in its wake.

What is the cause of all this confusion? Could it be that
we have cut ourselves off from learning at the source—the
liberal arts?

There is no need to exaggerate the symptoms of ill health

in American education. The facts speak for themselves. Here are a few of them, reduced to simple arithmetic:

In 1952–53 our total elementary school enrollment was 25 million and our secondary school enrollment 6.6 million (including, in both cases, both public and private schools). If the 1953 rate of increase should continue as expected, it would give us an elementary school enrollment of between 30 and 32 million by 1960, which would project itself into a secondary school enrollment of 11 to 12 million by 1965. How this in turn will affect our present higher education enrollment of about 2 million is not hard to imagine. It seems certain to increase it in proportion.

These trends have already created a shortage of classrooms which, despite our best efforts to date, stands at 325,000 and is expected to increase by another 425,000 by 1960. The results of this shortage are overcrowding, double and often triple sessions, fire and health hazards, and consequent deterioration in discipline and instruction.

Far worse is the shortage of teachers. Here we discover the alarming fact that in face of the rapidly increasing enrollment of students the supply of teachers is actually declining. The projected need for properly trained and qualified elementary school teachers in 1953 was 160,000, against which our colleges produced in 1952 only 36,000.

"The public has been repeatedly advised," declares the 1953 Teacher Supply and Demand Report of the National Education Association, "that the American school system is rapidly moving into a new era. The facts have been literally shouted from the housetops. . . . Yet scarcely anywhere is there evidence of adequate steps being taken to meet this crisis." Such conditions cannot fail to undermine the standards of both our liberal arts colleges and the graduate and professional schools of our universities and, through these, the cultural life, indeed the very security, of the nation.

It may seem a long way from these facts and figures to the traditional studies that have come down to us, through the medieval universities, from ancient Greece. It is a long way in time, but in cause and effect it is direct and short.

The obvious conclusion to draw from our facts is that we have allowed the population of the United States to out-race its educational resources. In quantitative terms we have permitted the demand to get far ahead of the supply, and we have turned our backs on the qualitative results. Why should this be so? We show no such indifference to our business cycle. Let its motion become erratic, and labor, management, government, the press are instantly alert. Why should we allow education to get the better of us?

There are many answers to this question, many reasons for our attitude, if no excuses for it. There is no reason more significant than the decline of the liberal arts as a force in our national educational system. These studies are disappearing under a layer of vocational and other substitutes like the landscape in the ice age, only this glacier reaches from coast to coast and border to border. With all due exceptions, and all honor and power to those exceptions, the attitude of most educational institutions toward this trend varies from mild concern to indifference and cheerful acquiescence.

Alas, no substitutes have been found for reading and writing. The practice and enjoyment of these skills in an ever widening orbit and on an ever ascending plane are both ends and means to the liberal arts. If deficiencies in the skills show up in colleges and even in the highly selective graduate schools of universities, do they not betray a comprehensive deficiency of the parent discipline?

The prevailing tendency is for the colleges to blame the schools for these deficiencies and for the schools to blame the colleges. Although primary responsibility rests with the schools—for liberal education must begin in secondary school if it is to take place at all—the colleges must bear their share of it. The liberal arts college, whether entirely independent or the mainspring of a complex university, that allows its curriculum to be penetrated in depth by such subjects as television, radio-listening, homemaking, basic communication skills, methods of study, beginning bowling, and story-telling (to cite a few concrete instances from the record); or that allows its athletes to major in physical education and gives them course credits for football, handball, elementary swimming, social dancing, rhythms, and fly fishing (to cite a few more) merely aids and abets such practices in the schools. It does little good for either to blame the other. The point is not which is more at fault. It is that both are denying themselves the benefits of studies which for two thousand years, throughout western civilization, have been esteemed as the key to the good life and all true academic achievement.

The point is substantiated by more disturbing evidence. While over half the nation's youth finishes high school and a fifth (of the whole) goes on to some form of higher education, this group includes less than half of those best qualified for such education. Of the top quarter in intellectual ability, 20 per cent do not continue for financial reasons and 40 per cent—a proportion exactly equal to that which does continue—for lack of motivation.

That so large a proportion of our best college material eschews higher education for such a reason is a fact that requires much interpretation. It is a composite of environment, chance, social status, geography, and other elements and influences. Is it not, too, further proof of our neglect of the liberal arts? The whole impulse and tendency of the liberal arts is to encourage the individual to make the most of all educational opportunities within reach and constantly to seek new ones. If the parents and teachers of these "unmotivated" young men and women had themselves been steeped in the liberal arts, would they not have communicated this impulse to their children and students? If their schools had afforded anything like proper introductions to the liberal arts, would the impulse have been lost?

The voluntary rejection of higher education by so many Americans capable of profiting by it shows that the grain cannot grow where the seed has not been planted. We can only speculate about how much talent is wasted in the process—certainly much that would bring strength and benefit to our society. This is another measure of the practical price society pays for its impractical evaluation of the liberal arts.

We are confused over the very meaning of the phrase, let alone the subjects of study for which it stands. It has acquired connotations of special privilege and preciosity. At the risk of laboring the obvious, therefore, let us recall that, as it is used here, the word "liberal" comes from the Latin *liber,* meaning "free"; that the proper meaning of the phrase "liberal arts" is "the arts becoming to a free man"; and that from earliest times these have included the sciences. (In the Middle Ages the liberal arts were arithmetic, geometry and astronomy, in addition to grammar, rhetoric, logic and music.) In other words, the liberal arts are rooted in freedom, not privilege, and they are broad, not narrow, in educational scope.

It is true that both Greek and medieval society restricted to a minority the number of those who were truly free, hence fully qualified as beneficiaries of the arts becoming a free man. In Greek times, these persons were the guardians of a fundamentally undemocratic society; in medieval times, aristocrats, clergy, and wandering scholars. It is also true that this identification of the liberal arts with special orders of society dies hard in modern Britain and Europe. It grew

out of a constricting interpretation of the meaning of freedom rather than a constriction inherent in the meaning of
the liberal arts, and it gained currency in the United States
through inverted snobbism as well as ignorance of the facts.
It is as much at variance with our cardinal principle of equal
opportunity as it is with the true meaning of the liberal arts.

The notion that the liberal arts are for the *rara avis* is no
less difficult to explain, though often more difficult to dispel.
Perhaps it is attributable to the rather narrow, literal meaning our workaday society attaches to the word "arts." Thus
the busy father discussing college with his son advises against
"impractical" courses that will not help him in business. Or
the scientist or engineer stresses professional purposes with
which he believes the liberal arts to be incompatible. In this
the champions of the liberal arts themselves have not been
altogether blameless. They have been guilty of smugness and
at times have seemed content to live on rote and reputation.

Such, for example, appears to have been the case in British
education in 1835 when Macaulay wrote in desperation:

> "Give a boy Robinson Crusoe. That is worth all the
> grammars of rhetoric and logic in the world . . . Who
> ever reasoned better for having been taught the differ-
> ence between a syllogism and an enthymeme? Who ever
> composed with greater spirit and elegance because he
> could define an oxymoron or an aposiopesis? I am not
> joking but writing quite seriously when I say that I
> would much rather order a hundred copies of Jack the
> Giant-Killer for our schools than a hundred copies of
> any grammar of rhetoric or logic that ever was written.

The same impatience with a curriculum whose claims were
pretentious but whose elements and purposes had become
obscure heralded the advent of the elective system in our
own schools and colleges half a century later.

All these impressions of the liberal arts rest upon a quantitative fallacy. They emphasize content as distinct from quality and spirit. If the critic reasons on this basis he may discount the liberal arts as severely as Dickens' Mr. Podsnap, who thought they should represent, reflect, and conduce to "getting up at eight, shaving close at a quarter-past, breakfasting at nine, going to the City at ten, coming home at half-past five, and dining at seven. Nothing else to be permitted to those same vagrants the Arts, on pain of excommunication." Or, evidently, as their exemplars were doing when Macaulay found them exuberating in oxymorons and enthymemes and voted for Robinson Crusoe. Or as the scientist does who forgets that science is part of the liberal arts; or the professional man who asks what Greek and Latin have to do with law or medicine or engineering.

The purpose of the liberal arts is not to teach business men business, or grammarians grammar, or college students Greek and Latin (which have disappeared from their required curricula). It is to awaken and develop the intellectual and spiritual powers in the individual before he enters upon his chosen career, so that he may bring to that career the greatest possible assets of intelligence, resourcefulness, judgment, and character.

It is, in John Stuart Mill's telling phrase, to make "capable and cultivated human beings." "Men are men," Mill said, "before they are lawyers or physicians or manufacturers; and if you make them capable and sensible men they will make themselves capable and sensible lawyers or physicians." I know of no better statement of the purpose of the liberal arts nor any that so firmly establishes their place in a national educational system that is dedicated, as ours is, to the preparation of men and women not just for intellectual pursuits but for life.

From this statement we may proceed as Mill himself did

to the conclusion that the liberal arts and many of the studies thought to be in competition with them are not competitors but allies. This was Mill's pronouncement on the conflict that raged in his day between the "old classical studies" and the "new scientific studies." Mill denied that this conflict had any foundation in principle whatsoever, declaring that "it is only the stupid inefficiency of the usual teaching which makes those studies be regarded as competitors instead of allies."

There is even less reason for such a conflict of principles today. The "old classical studies" have been greatly enriched by the infusion of history, philosophy, literature, language and the fine arts into the erstwhile domain of the grammarian and logician. The sciences never were "new" to the liberal arts, as they claimed three of the original seven. The social sciences—economics, anthropology, political science, sociology, psychology—have found their place in the sun alongside language and literature. The very term "liberal arts" has become synonymous with "liberal education," with its obviously broader implications of content and method. Every trade, profession, and vocation has an equal interest in "capable and cultivated human beings." How could this represent a conflict of principles?

It does not. The idea of a conflict of principle represents ignorance of the facts, with its usual by-products of misunderstanding and prejudice. That this is so should give us courage to attack these ancient enemies of learning. Though we cannot produce a magic formula that will relieve the shortages of schoolrooms and teachers, we can do a number of things that will contribute to those results.

Above all I would name two: first, we can maintain the liberal arts in the fullest possible health and vigor in our colleges, and second, we can capitalize them as a motivating force in American education by massive transfusions of the liberal arts into the training of secondary school teachers. Both steps would lead directly to improved conditions in the schools as well as in the colleges and universities. For of this I am convinced: that if this country is to be shaken out of the trance that blinds it to the needs of its educational system, the great awakening will be brought about by parents and teachers steeped in the liberal arts and imbued with their spirit.

Inhibiting all such measures, all progress, all hope of reform, is a profound misconception of the meaning of the word "practical." Let me illustrate.

It is said that because so many of our high school students (about 60 per cent) do not go on to college it would be impractical to introduce them to the liberal arts. This is to deny to a large segment of our society, which has already denied itself higher education, the only opportunity to benefit by such studies it is likely to have in its life. It is to ignore the possibility that half a loaf would be better than no loaf. Admitting wide variations in taste, aptitude, and intellectual competence among these students, is it "practical" to deny them their proportionate share of the richest experience education has to offer?

It is said that young men and women who move from high school directly into the labor force will have no time for such cultural opportunities as those opened up by the liberal arts. Yet the working week in American industry has shrunk to forty hours and is still shrinking. Who has more time on his hands than a modern factory worker? What does he do with it? Is it more "practical" to abandon him to his television and his comics or to hope that some past experience of the liberal arts, however brief, may impel him to further effort in self-education?

It is said that the demand for engineers is so urgent that it would be impractical to prolong their apprenticeship with the liberal arts. Yet the most urgent part of this urgent demand is for engineers who can cope with human problems. Only these can save our technology from becoming a headless, heartless, and eventually helpless monster. Is it "practical" to deny our engineers the educational opportunities they need to avert this disaster? Not philosophers alone but industrial executives and engineers themselves in increasing numbers are answering this question in the negative.

The same is true in the profession of medicine. What more "practical" profession is there than this, which so often holds, and must at all times be prepared to hold, the balance between life and death? The need for doctors is no less urgent than the need for engineers. The apprenticeship of doctors is the longest and hardest of any profession. It has been said, for these reasons, that it would be impractical to burden this apprenticeship with the liberal arts. Yet as medicine has enlarged its focus (and with it its curriculum) to include the behavioral with the natural sciences, and shifted its emphasis from the patient as a disease to the patient as a human being, it, too, has made articulate its demands for liberal education. Witness a recent resolution of the Association of American Medical Colleges favoring a broad, liberal education for premedical students.

What, in the last analysis, does "practical" mean? Does it mean "expedient"? Or does it mean that which accomplishes a given aim most fully and perfectly? I think it means the latter, and I hold by this meaning that it calls for a great awakening and a great revival of the liberal arts in American education.

What We Don't Know
Will Hurt Us

The conflict which rages around our schools is not a conflict between public and private institutions. It is a conflict between two different types of learning. Until we understand it as such, we are not likely to solve the many problems it involves—the acute shortage of teachers and schoolrooms, the financial exigencies, and the curricular confusion that fill the headlines.

Whatever the origin of this conflict, its tactics, polemics, and political pros and cons, its chief casualty has been the liberal arts. Yet of all learning, and to all learning, the wisest men of every generation—from the age of Pericles to the age of Eisenhower—have deemed these studies the most essential.

The liberal arts have constituted the basic studies from which all phases of the educational process—general, vocational, professional; elementary, secondary, and higher —draw nourishment and without which they languish and fail. Three hundred and fifty years ago, in the fifth century of Oxford and a quarter century before the founding of the first American university, Francis Bacon perceived this relationship and stated it as follows:

> First therefore, amongst so many great foundations
> of colleges in Europe I find it strange that they are all

17

dedicated to professions, and none left free to arts and sciences at large. For if men judge that learning should be referred to action, they judge well, but in this they fall into the error described in the ancient fable, in which the other parts of the body did suppose the stomach had been idle, because it neither performed the office of motion, as the limbs do, nor of sense, as the head doth, but yet notwithstanding it is the stomach that digesteth and distributeth to all the rest. So if any man think philosophy and universality to be idle studies, he doth not consider that all professions are from thence served and supplied. And this I take to be a great cause that hath hindered the progression of learning, because these fundamental knowledges have been studied but in passage. For if you will have a tree bear more fruit than it hath used to do, it is not any thing you can do to the boughs, but it is the stirring of the earth and putting new mould about the roots that must work it.

No one since Bacon has improved upon his statement of the case.

Why has it been so difficult for us to perceive the role of the liberal arts? One reason is the nature of the controversy in which American education is now involved. A second Battle of the Books is in progress—and, as in the first, the "quarrel is so inflamed by the warm heads of either faction, and the pretensions somewhere or other so exorbitant, as not to admit the least overtures of accommodation." At times the quarrel seems as pointless as Englishmen criticizing Germans for not speaking English, or golfers ridiculing tennis players for playing tennis with rackets instead of golf sticks. There is an exchange of invective but no exchange of meaning.

This quarrel has confused the issue. The adversaries in

Swift's satire were ancient versus modern learning, as Swift knew them at the end of the seventeenth century. At first glance, today's adversaries would seem to be their lineal descendants: the same Ancients (who by now have recruited most of Swift's Moderns including Swift himself) versus the Moderns of 1954. A closer look reveals that this is not precisely the case. It would appear from the polemics that the Ancients were now opposed by a wholly different adversary known as instrumentalism, which sprang full-flowered from the brow of John Dewey and entered the lists against classical learning barely half a century ago. It would seem that most of the troubles or triumphs of American education (depending upon how one looks at them) had resulted from the application of this brand-new American invention to the educational process.

Such an oversimplification of history distorts the educational problem and hinders its solution. Granting the considerable (and demonstrable) influence of Mr. Dewey and his followers on our educational system, particularly upon our schools of education, teachers' colleges, and public schools, it has been but one of many historical forces that have contributed to the present situation.

Let us look more closely at today's Battle of the Books. If its adversaries are not logical counterparts of Swift's, what are they? They are proponents of two different types of learning which have existed and competed with one another since ancient times—not as old versus new, but as two distinct sets of purposes and methods. The purposes and methods of the liberal arts were first defined by the Greeks. They are expounded in the writings of Plato and Aristotle; and though they have passed through ancient, medieval, and modern phases, they still retain their original meaning. They are not a body of revealed truths or logical absolutes or a quantum of knowledge. They are studies designed to develop to capacity the intellectual and spiritual powers of the individual. Their aim is to make the most of a man in order that he may make the most of his calling, his cultural opportunities, and his responsibilities as a citizen. Such was the meaning of the liberal arts in Plato's time and such is it today.

Instrumentalism is just as old as the liberal arts and fundamentally just as consistent in meaning. In current usage, instrumentalism has become a synonym for pragmatism, especially as applied to education. Essentially it means the identification of truth with utility. That is true or good which works, which accomplishes results, or which gives emotional satisfaction to the believer.

"The true, to put it very briefly," William James once wrote in a summary of pragmatism, "is only the expedient in the way of thinking, just as the 'right' is only the expedient in the way of our behaving. Expedient in almost any fashion; and expedient in the long run and on the whole, of course."

These words should not be read out of moral context. Both James and Dewey believed that immorality, even according to traditional standards, would be found in expedient. But the words forge a link with the Sophists of the fifth century B.C., whose slogan was "Man is the measure of all things" and whose intensely practical instruction in law, rhetoric, or—in the case of the versatile Hippias—almost any trade, emphasized the subjective desires of their pupils and their satisfaction in utilitarian skills and occupations.

I leave for the moment the relative merits of these two educational philosophies. Liberal education has periodically dried up in formalism and is never proof against illiberal teaching. Bacon himself takes certain contemporary Cambridge professors to task for teaching "words and not matter." Form without substance, polish without purpose, have always been a "distemper of learning" to the liberal arts. If we think of utilitarian education in the sense of occupational training, we will find that it has always had a respectable place in society; it had such a place in the medieval guild system; it has it in our secondary schools today.

If, on the other hand, we think of it in the sense of instrumentalism, this too has made useful contributions to the educational process, especially at the level of elementary education. My point, however, is not the respective merits of liberal and utilitarian education but their common antiquity. Once this is appreciated, the present dispute assumes its true character. It is not a dispute between Ancients and Moderns, or tradition and invention. It is a dispute between two Ancients which has been going on a long time.

Another thing the Sophists and instrumentalists have in common is that each arose in answer, as it were, to a specific set of practical demands. All philosophy reflects its times, in language and metaphor if not in theory. Even Plato, with his insistence upon the independent reality of ideas, was sensitive to the conditions in which he lived. But while Plato towered over his times, the Sophists fitted into them as hand into glove. The Sophists were a group of professional teachers who responded to the demands of young men for practical education that would help them get ahead in the world. Some of these young men were members of a rising plutocracy and anxious for instruction in the ways of democracy. Others were just looking for careers, uninterested in philosophy and the arts but eager to learn a trade. To all of these demands the Sophists responded with a body of teachings and a point of view so congenial to modern pragmatism that Schiller, the English pragmatist, called himself their disciple. For all the latter-day strictures upon them, their teachings flourished in the same society that sustained Plato and Aristotle.

Pragmatism made its modern appearance in the United States toward the close of the nineteenth century and in the early years of the twentieth in the writings of C. S. Peirce, William James, and John Dewey. These were the years in which the United States was passing through a highly self-conscious phase of nationalism that expressed itself in our war with Spain and a short-lived flurry of imperialism. Business was booming, and obsessing our thoughts and energies to a degree unparalleled in history. These trends were accompanied by an exuberant nativism that strove for expression in our cultural life. Ties with the past, and with older civilizations, were being cut. Optimism, improvisation, and Americanism were the order of the day. It is hard to conceive of a doctrine more perfectly suited to these conditions and attitudes than pragmatism.

Much the same can be said of pragmatism in the form of instrumentalism as Dewey and his followers applied it to our schools. The first half of the present century saw changes in the character and composition of our schools, particularly our secondary schools; this doctrine was ideally suited to accommodate them. Because of the decisive part secondary education plays in liberal education—which must begin in high school if it is to begin at all—it will repay us to consider some of these changes in detail. To sum them up, they produced, as though from dragon's teeth, an enormous new secondary school population, most of which was entirely innocent of the liberal arts and their purposes. The demand placed upon our schools for the kind of utilitarian education that the young Athenians demanded of the Sophists was overwhelming. The schools rose to meet the demand with the ancient doctrine of instrumentalism.

The brunt of this new educational burden was borne by our public secondary schools. Compulsory school-attendance laws and child-labor laws gradually accumulated throughout the states, with the effect of keeping in school boys and girls who used to quit after the eighth grade. As automatic machinery developed and the labor market became more crowded, labor union policies had the same effect. The appeal of secondary education—whether for some vocation, for life, or, via higher education, for a profession—became more positive and more popular. As college degrees became standard requirements for entrance into the professions and all but standard for many types of business, high school diplomas acquired a similar if lesser material value. Meanwhile, as a force in itself and a prime mover behind all these laws and policies, the population of the United States rose from 76,000,000 to 150,000,000.

The results of these trends reveal themselves in three dramatic sets of figures. From 1910 to 1940 the percentage of the 14- to 15-year age group in the nation's labor force declined from 30 per cent to 5 per cent. The percentage of the 17-year age group enrolled in high school rose from 30 per cent to 60 per cent; and the total high school population increased from 1,111,000 to 7,113,000. The comparable increase of enrollment in elementary education in these three decades was from 18,450,000 to 21,050,000. In other words, while elementary school enrollment increased by less than one-sixth, high school increased by more than six times. From 1900 to 1950 it rose from around 10 per cent to 75 per cent of its age group. What this amounted to was the creation, almost overnight, of a huge new educational population.

In curricular preference this population was overwhelmingly vocational. A disproportionately large part of it consisted of the children of immigrants. These immigrants poured into the country in such numbers in the first quarter of the century (over a million a year for six of the years between 1900 and 1920) that their total number together with their children reached a peak of 38,000,000. At no time between 1900 and 1950 was it below 25,000,000. In 1920, for example, it stood at 35,000,000, exactly a third of our total population of 105,000,000.

The overwhelming majority of this group of immigrant and recent immigrant origin lacked even a smattering of liberal education or comprehension of its purposes. Allowing for exceptions—more numerous among certain national and cultural groups than among others—the typical immigrant of these years was a person of humble origin and circumstances who had been denied access to liberal education by the highly selective educational systems prevailing abroad. How therefore could he be expected to understand it and transmit its motivations to his children? If he had ever thought of the liberal arts at all, the chances are it was as one of the aristocratic class privileges which he had come to America to escape. I know that with some it worked the other way, and that among these men and women are some of the staunchest supporters of liberal education the country has ever had. But the rank and file were innocents.

It was precisely this group, moreover, that the child-labor and school-attendance laws forced into our high schools in greatest numbers, since it was from them that so much of our unskilled and semi-skilled factory labor was recruited. Schools take their character not only from their pupils but from parents, whether the parental influence (or lack of it) stems from home, parent-teachers' association, ballot-box, or school board. The schools cannot set and maintain standards unless parents understand and support them. My point is not that our foreign population opposed

24

liberal education. It is that through lack of previous op-portunity they failed to comprehend it and therefore failed to support it. We may weigh the effect of this failure upon the liberal arts by asking ourselves what the effect on curriculum might have been if they all had been graduates of European universities; or American colleges; or, for that matter, of American public high schools of an earlier generation.

Our immigrant population was not the only such weight in these scales. Among our native population fifteen million Negro citizens, heretofore lacking any but the most primitive educational opportunities, became rightful claimants to the benefits of secondary education. For want of previous opportunity they too lacked comprehension of the liberal arts. In 1920 their number was 10,400,000. If we add this to the number of foreign-born and their children in that year, it gives us a total of 45,000,000 out of 105,000,000 Americans, beyond the pale, so to speak, of the liberal arts.

Nor does this complete the total. Liberal education characteristically begins where elementary education leaves off and carries through to the end of college. A recent study places the most critical phase of liberal education in the last two years of secondary school and the first two years of college. Certain it is that a heavy share of responsibility for it devolves upon secondary education, not only in its curriculum but in disseminating a general awareness of its purposes and benefits through society. In 1900 barely 10 per cent of its age group finished high school. Millions of native white citizens sent their children to high school in the years that followed with no idea of what liberal education was and no encouragement from home to find out. The frontiersman's hostility toward book learning was still strong. Materialism was rampant. Plunkitt of Tammany Hall spoke with scorn of "college professors and philosophers who go up in a balloon to think"; and the voice of Plunkitt was the voice of the nation.

Is it any wonder that in this suddenly expanded realm of secondary education, where from time immemorial the liberal arts have had to prove themselves in competition with utilitarian education of all kinds—where they have always had to make a case for themselves or give ground— they gave ground? They did not give it in an objective test of merit or by decision of policy. They gave it by default.

No matter how or why the ground was given, it was a serious setback to education in general. Its seriousness can be measured not merely in hypothetical conjectures about human happiness but in concrete losses of manpower. These show up vividly in studies of the number and type of high school graduates entering college today. From such studies two telling facts appear. The first is that of the 25 per cent of our high school graduates best qualified for higher educa- tion, 40 per cent do not continue with it for lack of motiva- tion. The second fact is that most of these intellectually competent yet unmotivated young men and women come from homes representing the cultural groups and attitudes we have been discussing. How great a loss we have sustained by this wastage of human talent we can only surmise.

Could the schools have provided a better understanding of the liberal arts, through their own teachers and curric- ula, in spite of all the cultural odds against them? To have done so they would have needed, first, much more specific and powerful assistance from parents; but the parental tendency was to default responsibilities to the schools and then criticize the schools for not discharging them. The result was to force into both liberal and vocational cur- ricula subjects previously treated in the home or (at times) behind the woodshed. The increasing secularization of American life contributed to the same result, causing both home and church to look to the schools for moral discipline. And to these new burdens, government added its demand for training in citizenship. The whole imposed upon the schools a crude lay morality of "life adjustment" which their hard-pressed teachers made shift to impart in the classroom —to the common loss of the liberal arts and of really useful occupational training.

To have resisted or modified these trends, the schools would have needed, secondly, much greater financial support than was forthcoming, particularly for teachers' salaries. I know this is an old story and that it is sometimes exaggerated—that it has perhaps even been used as an excuse for not undertaking educational reforms which could at least have been started without money. But as I write these very words, my morning paper carries the headline, "Teacher Scarcity at Critical Stage," and a report from the President of the American Association of School Administrators that our average annual teacher salary is $3,600, "with large numbers getting $2,000 or less." There is a direct cause-and-effect relationship between the salary and the headline. The report goes on to recommend the spending of $26,600,000,000 for school buildings during the next six years. I do not mean to labor this all-too-familiar argument. Yet no explanation of our educational predicament can possibly ignore it. We have the resources to solve this financial problem. A stronger representation of the liberal arts among teachers and students as well as among parents, school boards, and taxpayers would expedite its solution.

To have put forth a greater effort in the interest of liberal education, the schools would have needed, finally, much more specific—and sympathetic—assistance from the liberal arts colleges and universities than they received—particularly from the universities. In the nineteenth century there was institutional as well as intellectual continuity between the secondary and higher phases of liberal education. To preserve this continuity, two things are required above all others. These are, first, the closest possible cooperation between school and college in such matters as the planning of curriculum and the testing and guidance of students; and, second, both secondary school and college teachers aware of and prepared for these responsibilities. In the nineteenth century such continuity was ensured, partly by the liberal arts curricula prevailing generally throughout our secondary schools and partly by the fact that these schools recruited their teachers almost entirely from the liberal arts colleges.

Toward the turn of the century this continuity began to be disrupted. It is difficult to say exactly how the disruption started, but the colleges and universities were at least partly to blame. As the elective system gained headway in the colleges, liberal education lost character and in extreme cases became so dissipated as to be hardly recognizable. In part the elective system was the result of European (particularly German) influence that emphasized specialization culminating in graduate work. In even larger part it resulted from the deficiencies of the liberal arts themselves, from their failure to keep fresh and vital and reveal their meaning to their own disciples. It began in the 1870's, a good thirty years before Dewey published his *School and Society*.

By disrupting the unity of the liberal arts on a horizontal plane the elective system greatly abetted the disruption of their continuity on a vertical plane. The result in curricular terms was a tide rip of vocational and liberal currents. The liberal arts colleges—partly out of conviction and partly in deference to the professional schools and the professions—continued to offer liberal education, however diluted by vocational and other electives, and to require preparation in the liberal arts on the part of entering freshmen. The schools met this requirement with a curricular mixture of liberal, vocational, and life-adjustment courses in which the liberal element became steadily more diluted.

The results are epitomized in a letter which I have before me. It contains the transcript of a high school senior applying for admission to the liberal arts curriculum of Yale University. The transcript shows that of twelve junior and senior courses offered as the first half of the liberal arts continuum, two were in English, one in American history, and the other nine were as follows: typing, speech, (2) chorus, (2) physical education, journalism, personality problems, and marriage and family. The subjects required, in varying combination, for admission to Yale are English language and literature, two foreign languages, mathematics, history, and the natural sciences. An answer frequently given me to the question raised by this obvious conflict is that the student should not have been allowed to apply for Yale. A more satisfactory answer would be that his innate aptitude and competence should have been discovered in time for his high school to assign him to those studies which would have made his admission to Yale possible.

The gap in the continuity of liberal education between school and college grew wider when the liberal arts faculties in the universities relinquished responsibility for the training of secondary school teachers to special schools and departments of education in the universities and to the newly founded teachers' colleges. This is not to suggest that the liberal arts were willfully suppressed or utterly forsaken. On the contrary they struck new roots in the teachers' colleges, in some of which they flourished—and continue to flourish—more than in some so-called liberal arts institutions. It is to say, rather, that what might have been a united effort became a divided one, which had lost the support of its strongest potential ally, the liberal arts faculties of the universities.

This process, which in its early stages appears to have been largely involuntary, was abetted by the demand for teachers that was caused by the soaring high school enroll-ment. It was further abetted by the comparably increas-ing need for university and college teachers, and the grow-ing concern of the liberal arts faculties with that need. The relatively unfavorable working conditions, compensation, and intellectual opportunities of high school teaching also played a part.

Here again liberal education lost ground by default. The sad part of it is that what began as an involuntary and almost imperceptible schism culminated in an acrimony and a second Battle of the Books. It is not necessary to become embroiled in the battle to recognize the harmful effect of this dissidence on liberal education. To prepare for in-struction in one set of values and purposes formerly repre-sented by one faculty, there were now two faculties—one passive, the other active, with conflicting purposes. What should have been a colloquium turned into a conflict in which no one gained and liberal education was the heavy loser.

The liberal arts faculties of the universities did not want this conflict and did not start it. It is simply a rather more acute manifestation than usual of the ancient competition between two kinds of learning. If, in this conflict, the lib-eral arts faculties have been more sinned against than sin-ning, they too did some sinning.

My conclusion from all these facts is that the schools did not receive the support in liberal education they needed from the colleges and universities to uphold their end of the bargain.

The entire country has been the loser and the entire

country is responsible for its own loss. The educational process is indivisible. Each part of it depends upon every other part. If we single out the universities as standard-bearers we must not forget that these standards, too, require the support of parents—a cultural base of comprehension and sympathy—or they cannot be maintained. If the truth be told, there was little comprehension of the power of the liberal arts in American society because American society was incurious and inarticulate concerning its own political and social philosophy. Not since the great days of the Federal Convention, the Federalist Papers, the writings and teachings of Adams and Jefferson, and the seminal decisions of John Marshall had we bothered to inquire much into the meaning of our democracy and the vital part of it represented by liberal education. The glow of that early enlightenment soon faded in the American sky, and while we remained furiously awake in business and politics, in philosophy we went to sleep. We were not roused from this sleep and impelled to re-examine first principles until economic collapse, followed by the threat of fascist and then of communist totalitarianism, forced us to look into the meaning of many things we had taken for granted. Then and only then (and I speak of the last two decades) did we begin to discover the meaning that liberal education held for Plato and Aristotle and Adams and Jefferson.

No one was more sympathetic to education in all its phases than Jefferson. He spoke constantly of "a general diffusion of knowledge" as the corollary to self-government; and he made comprehensive plans which included vocational as well as liberal education. He believed that all Americans should be taught "reading, writing, and common arithmetic"; that all should learn some useful trade or calling; and that all who had the ability should go just as far in higher education as their ability permitted them; and he saw no incompatibility between these three principles. At the same time, as his personal correspondence and the whole record of his life reveal, it was liberal education that enriched his own mind and spirit and through them conveyed transcendent benefits to all American education.

The same can be said of Lincoln, who had almost no formal education and whose discovery and use of liberal education for this very reason offers a truly pragmatic demonstration of its powers. "It was a wild region," he wrote in 1859 of Spencer County, Indiana, whither his uneducated father moved the family from Kentucky in Lincoln's eighth year, "with many bears and other wild animals, still in the woods."

> There I grew up. There were some schools, so called; but no qualification was ever required of a teacher beyond "readin, writin, and cipherin" to the Rule of Three. If a straggler supposed to understand latin happened to sojourn in the neighborhood, he was looked upon as a wizzard (*sic*). There was absolutely nothing to excite ambition for education. Of course when I came of age I did not know much. . . . I could read, write and cipher to the Rule of Three; but that was all. I have not been to school since. The little advance I now have upon this store of education, *I have picked up from time to time under the pressure of necessity.*

Whither did this practical motive lead him? It led him to English grammar at the age of twenty-three; to Euclid when he was a member of Congress; to the Bible; to Bunyan, Shakespeare, Defoe, Burns, and Byron; to Blackstone's *Commentaries;* to American history; to Voltaire, Gibbon, and Paine. It led him, in short, to liberal education, and this in turn led on to greater things.

Was it Lincoln's genius or his education that took him the rest of the way? It was both. He was no towering intellectual. The nature of his genius was that he so perfectly represented the ideals and aspirations of his country and his fellow men. Without this education he might have continued to represent those ideals and aspirations in the back woods of Illinois. With the help of a liberal education he represented them, and not only represented but advanced and strengthened them, for the world. What liberal education offered Lincoln in his time, a proper diffusion of its power through our educational system offers us all today.

We neglect this knowledge at our peril.

Better Men *and*
Better Mousetraps

The scholar has been a long time finding himself in the United States. More than a century has passed since Emerson, in "The American Scholar," identified him as Man Thinking, man living and improving his life by the use of his intellectual powers, and made him welcome in the name of a "revolution . . . to be wrought by the gradual domestication of the idea of Culture." The frontier has been conquered. Colleges and universities are spread in profusion from coast to coast. American art, music, science, law, and letters are also known to the world that consumes our movies and our soft drinks. Yet the scholar still spends precious hours in the wastelands, not as the prodigal who has wandered from his home, but as the pioneer who has not yet found it, or who, having found it, is not yet sure of his title and deed. What are his prospects?

Man Thinking seems up against it in an age that has carried specialization and the division of labor far beyond the wildest dreams of Adam Smith. If Emerson could think of American society in 1837 as "one in which the members have suffered amputation from the trunk" and man is "metamorphosed into a thing, into many things," what would he say of it today? In his more familiar lineaments as the member of a university faculty, the scholar seems hard put to it to justify his calling to his countrymen.

There is more than money at the heart of this matter. Again and again surveys and conference reports emphasize the need of raising the prestige of teaching as well as the salaries. This is but another way of confessing our failure as a people to perceive the connection between teaching and scholarship and to understand scholarship as a basic function of civilized society. Our "long apprenticeship to the learning of other lands" which Emerson saw drawing to a close has come to a close. But the "revolution . . . to be wrought by the gradual domestication of the idea of Culture" has not yet fulfilled itself. We have created an American culture in which, for all its shortcomings, we may take pride, but we persist in denying its strength to our scholars and their strength to it.

But, we may say, have the labors of our university faculties not been fruitful? Has not American scholarship survived economic collapse, social upheaval, and three great wars? It has, of course, and strange as it may seem grown stronger in the process. Yet there is a difference between these experiences and the circumstances confronting it today. What it has survived, even benefited from, is adversity, a perverse but ancient friend to learning. What it suffers from today is delusion, its mortal foe. American scholarship went hungry in Emerson's day for lack of sustenance. Today it starves amid plenty.

Various and unreliable is our use of the word "scholar." We call an accommodating friend (or stranger) a gentleman and a scholar. We say of an academic colleague that he has given up teaching for scholarship, or vice versa, as if they were two different things. Or we translate scholarship into quantitative terms, through the number of books and articles published rather than what they say, or through the various quantitative measurements applied in the practice of institutional accreditation. Alternately, the scholar is pedant, bookworm, antiquarian, eccentric, misanthrope, a queer, cantankerous, carping individual out of sorts with society and ill at ease with himself; or the very acme and essence of gregariousness, the holder of a so-called athletic scholarship and the darling of the coliseum crowds. We find him, too, the butt of his intellectual peers, the book reviewers, their stock model of all that is awful in literary style; and we see him, complete with his badge of authority, the Doctorate of Philosophy, engaged in pedagogical activities to which no true philosopher would stoop, even to conquer.

The master delusion, the parent of all these fantasies, is the idea of the scholar as The Intellectual, a being apart from his fellow men, a snob, a mystic, the ineffable member of an ineffable, and to ordinary mortals unattainable, caste. Thus we speak of the role of The Intellectual in America instead of the role of the intellect, of anti-intellectualism as a hue-and-cry after a group of individuals instead of forces inhibiting the use of the intellect.

The scholar is not The Intellectual. He is Man Thinking. Man Thinking is not the member of a race apart. He is the citizen performing the function appointed for all citizens in a civilized state, a function without which there would be no civilized state. He is Everyman purposefully apprehending the meaning of things. Granted that there are degrees of competence in this art, as there are in all arts, and that its practice is, like all arts, primarily an individual affair, it is in no sense snobbish or antisocial. The right to practice it is part of the birthright of all men and the need is the need of all. We would do much better, I think, to seek it out as such rather than as the personification of a special privilege or the esoteric monopoly of a few. By liberating the scholar in all of us we shall create a reservoir

to relieve our teacher shortages while our hunt for Intellectuals loses itself in the desert.

I must now defend the proposition that the scholar is a
teacher. In Emerson's definition, I do not see how he can
help being one. No matter how silent or inarticulate he is,
how much inclined to keep his thoughts to himself, he
generates currents that he cannot contain. "Nature provided for the communication of thought by planting with
it in the receiving mind a fury to impart it," says Emerson
in one of his later essays. " 'Tis so in every art, in every
science. One burns to tell the new fact, the other burns to
hear it." The scholarly impulse is present in all parties to
the educational process. Between the true scholar and the
teacher there is no fundamental incompatibility but a fundamental affinity of the most intimate kind.

How many potential teachers lie asleep in the deluded
giant of American scholarship? Many more, I think, than
we imagine. Enough to bring substantial relief to our hard-
pressed educational institutions, from the greatest universities to the loneliest rural schools. What will free them
and put them to work? The conferences have not disturbed
their slumber. Money will help in salaries that make possible a decent living, but money has never been the scholar's
main incentive. Again I suggest that we turn our attention
to other incentives, not in a counsel of despair because the
funds for improving his salary are lacking, but because I
think this the most likely way of expediting their appro-
priation; and further, because without these other incentives the funds themselves will not suffice. To bring our
inquiry within manageable compass, let me put the question, What can we do in our colleges and universities now,
without reference to funds, to further the cause of scholarship as I have defined it and relieve our teacher shortages
by this means?

37

Let us return once more to Emerson to see whither his thoughts may lead us along this path. To him the three great influences upon the mind of the scholar were nature, books, and action. Emerson was too much the individualist and the poet to take much interest or repose much faith in the details of a college curriculum. Beyond the expressed hope (in "The American Scholar") that his country would "fill the postponed expectation of the world with something better than the exertions of mechanical skill," the conviction that our colleges and universities were essential to the fulfillment of that expectation, and a few fragments in his Journal embodying the classic components of the liberal arts, he leaves the scholar's precise academic regime largely to inference. But his concept of the scholar did have curricular implications. The ends he sought, the aesthetic and philosophical standards he set for Man Thinking, not to mention his own reading and study, all bespeak scholarship as a process of discovery and renewal that required its proper food. The thought is encouraging. For if the academic counterpart of the right attitude toward scholarship is the right curriculum for the scholar, it should be within our power to do something about that forthwith.

The belief that certain kinds of learning offer a greater incentive to Man Thinking than certain other kinds is an ancient one. It comes down to us in unbroken tradition from the pages of Plato and Aristotle. The latter opens his "Ethics" with a discourse in which, while conceding that all arts aim at the good, he points out that some have manifold ends, as health is to medicine, whereas others are of a "single capacity," such as bridle-making. Among all of these, he says, "the ends of the master arts are to be preferred to all the subordinate ends; for it is for the sake of the former that the latter are pursued." Plato propounded the same principle, which Socrates illustrates in the

"Gorgias" in a discourse on cooking and medicine:

> cookery in my opinion is only an experience, and not
> an art at all; and . . . whereas medicine is an art, and
> attends to the nature and constitution of the patient,
> and has principles of action and reason in each case,
> cookery in attending upon pleasure never regards
> either the nature or reason of that pleasure to which
> she devotes herself, but goes straight to her end, nor
> ever considers or calculates anything, but works by
> experience and routine, and just preserves the recol-
> lection of what she has usually done when producing
> pleasure. . . . I would have you consider . . . whether
> there are not other similar processes which have to
> do with the soul—some of them processes of art,
> making a provision for the soul's highest interest—
> others despising the interest, and, as in the previous
> case, considering only the pleasure of the soul, and
> how this may be acquired, but not considering what
> pleasures are good or bad, and having not other aim
> but to afford gratification, whether good or bad.

No one strove more earnestly to translate this belief in
a differentiation of value among the kinds of learning into
the precise subject matter of higher education than Cardinal Newman. A resemblance of his "man of philosophic
habit" to Emerson's Man Thinking appears in the chief
attribute Newman ascribes to the former, namely "the
power of viewing many things at once as one whole, of
referring them severally to their true place in the universal
system, of understanding their respective values and determining their mutual dependence."

The curriculum Newman propounds in his "Idea of a
University" is the one he deems most conducive to that

power. It consists primarily of learning which has *intrinsic* value—that is, learning whose attainment and possession enlarges and ennobles the mind and is therefore valuable in itself, as distinct from learning which has *extrinsic* value —that is, learning whose value can be realized only from its application and use. Although Newman, like Plato and Aristotle before him, does not rule the latter type of learning out if it also possesses intrinsic value, he makes this the test, and he insists that even such learning as possesses both values should be studied for its intrinsic value. Such was his ideal for the university he founded in Dublin and for the man of philosophic habit, its ideal graduate. Some of these ideals he derived from his study of the Greek and Roman philosophers; some he derived empirically as student and fellow at Oxford; and some he created as a man of philosophic habit himself. If the ideals never fully materialized, Newman's championship of them gave them renewed vigor and force.

Such a renewal has taken place in every generation from Plato's to ours that has seriously put its mind to the question. Why should it not take place today? For centuries we have disputed among ourselves over the different kinds of learning, and the prospect is that the dispute will go merrily on *ad infinitum*. Should that prevent us from giving freer rein to the kind of learning which the weight of historical experience and the preponderance of philosophical testimony both argue offers the greatest incentive to Man Thinking? This is something each one of us can attend to in his own college or university. How much more profitable it might be than drafting pious resolutions at conferences and waiting about for nonexistent funds.

If our quest of true scholarship should lead us to a definition of the true university, so much the better. But I doubt whether we can hurry this process. American usage is against us, as in the long run both British and Irish usage were against Newman. No matter what our ancestors meant by the word "university," it has come to mean so many things to us that I think it unlikely we shall ever achieve complete consistency of meaning or uniformity of standards in our use of it. One thing we can do, however. We can have done with the notion that there is no essential difference between the kinds of learning in our colleges, that one kind is as good as another regardless of what if any meaning we attribute to the word "good."

Our whole national tradition is rooted in the idea that our people shall receive instruction in both learning of intrinsic and learning of extrinsic value and make the most of both, each according to his competence. This tradition was founded by men steeped in learning of intrinsic value, Aristotle's "master arts," Plato's "provision for the soul's highest interest," Newman's "power of viewing many things at once as one whole," the chief incentive and inspiration of the scholar both as student and as teacher for 2,000 years. Out of this kind of learning came the most hopeful system of education any nation has yet conceived. Why should we allow that system's hopes to lag when we could revive them by refreshing them at their source? We have neglected pure learning. We have even slighted the *invention* of better mousetraps to bestow our honors upon their *mass production*. We need them all—the pure learning, the practical inventiveness, and the mechanical skill—but we need them in proportion to their values if we are to save our civilization and our souls.

The American scholar is not Faust at his black magic or a gypsy in flight from his fellow men or a man of philosophical habit caught in a philosophical vise. He is Man Thinking, hungering and thirsting after the things that make man think. We have those things at our disposal. Let us give them to him, for our own sake as well as for his, but especially for the sake of our teaching profession.

Time to Repair
the Bridge

It is now generally recognized throughout the United States that our high schools are not performing adequately one of the two main functions they are supposed to perform in our educational system. This is the function of a bridge between elementary school and college. Whatever they may be accomplishing in the preparation for citizenship of students who do not go on to college—and there is widespread dissatisfaction with that, too—as bridges to higher education they are buckling in the middle.

Less than half of the top quarter of our high school graduates, the group best qualified for college education, move on into it. The rest drop out of the procession largely for sheer lack of motive: they fail to see the purpose of an education commensurate with their native talents and ability. Others of the same academic potential follow lines of least resistance and do not make their way to the top of their high school classes. Still others, of less ability and lower potential, drift into public institutions obliged to admit them, only to fall by the wayside as soon as they encounter bona fide university standards. Even among the top quarter of high school graduates there are too many instances of ground lost to inadequate preparation in particular subjects that has to be made up in the freshman year of college at the cost of more valuable educational opportunities.

Sometimes this ground is not regained until much later, if ever. Witness the recent recommendation of the Association of Graduate Schools that an examination in basic command of the English language be required for admission to those schools. That the graduate schools of our universities should find such a requirement necessary for candidates for the Ph.D., the highest earned academic degree awarded in the United States, is striking evidence of shortcomings farther down the educational line. The foundations of basic command of our native language, the essential tool for all learning, should be laid in grammar school and completed in high school. The time for this test is at the beginning of college, not the end of it.

All this constitutes a waste of the most precious of all our natural resources—our human resources—and this at a time when we are wondering how, or even whether, we can keep up with the Russians and are calling for "talent hunts" and "brain-power quests" to assist us. Meanwhile we are informed by such authorities as the United States Office of Education and the Educational Policies Commission of the National Education Association and the American Association of School Administrators that the Russians are investing substantially more time, money, and energy in grammar schools and high schools as a preparation for college education than we are. This follows from the fact that the proportion of Russia's total national income allocated to education is reportedly 17 per cent as compared to 5 per cent in our own case. Students in the Russian schools complete in ten years what ours do in twelve (spending an average of 1,089 hours in school in each of their last four years, compared with our average of 895). A considerably larger proportion of them are enrolled in the academic curriculum than is the case with us; and, although a reduction in that proportion appears to be in prospect, what is more to the point is that within their academic curricu-

43

lum, such basic subjects as language, literature, mathematics, and the natural sciences receive much greater emphasis and attention than they do in our own. Russian language and literature occupy 28 per cent of that curriculum; history, nearly 7 per cent; geography, 5 per cent; foreign language, 7 per cent; mathematics, 20 per cent; biology, physics, and chemistry together, 13 per cent.

"The emphasis on science in Soviet schools contrasts sharply with the situation in the United States," says the United States Office of Education in its 1957 report, *Education in the U.S.S.R.*

"Whereas the Soviet students graduating from secondary schools in June 1955 had taken courses in physics for five years, astronomy for one year, chemistry for four years, biology for five years and mathematics, algebra, geometry, and trigonometry for ten years, less than a third of the American high school graduates had taken a year of chemistry, about a fourth had had a year of physics, and less than a seventh had taken advanced mathematics."

Although the Russian science courses are not, in all cases, full-year courses, it is nevertheless true that every Russian ten-year-school graduate will have had 4.4 full years of mathematics and 5.9 full years of science. The Office of Education also reports that in Russia all students in the ten-year schools (whose last three years roughly equate with our four-year high schools) are required to study foreign languages for six years, whereas less than 15 per cent of our high school students study any foreign language and most of these for not more than a year.

We may draw various conclusions from the Russian system of grammar and high school education. The almost complete repression of freedom that accompanies it undoubtedly limits the ultimate benefits it might confer upon Russian society, especially in the fields of the humanities and the social sciences, where freedom of thought is of the essence. We may question the distribution of emphasis in the curriculum and ask whether such a stiff dose of science in secondary school will yield all the results that are expected of it. Nevertheless, we may safely conclude two things. The first is that any student who completes satisfactorily as much mathematics and foreign language study as the Russian academic curriculum requires should have a better-disciplined mind than his American counterpart, whatever he may do with it. The second is that any student who has completed as much foreign language study together with the study of his own language and literature as the Russian curriculum requires should have a better mastery of both than does his American counterpart. These facts, added to the obviously stronger foundation for proficiency in science and technology afforded by the Russian curriculum, make the weaknesses in our own curriculum seem all the more glaring.

For more than a decade critics of American education have been trying in vain to open our eyes to the existence of these weaknesses. The Russian *deus ex machina* has succeeded in accomplishing what they could not accomplish. Like the great depression that shocked us out of the illusions we held with respect to our economy in 1930, and the bombing of Pearl Harbor that shocked us out of illusions regarding our military security and our position in world affairs in 1941, the sudden revelation of Russia's scientific advance has at last shocked us out of our educational illusions. Though scarcely visible to the human eye, the two Sputniks have bathed our high school curriculum in a flood of light and magnified the voice of its critics into a national chorus.

This is not a wholly unmixed blessing. To be sure, the first step toward correcting any fault is to recognize it. But there is now so much criticism of our high schools from so many points of view, surcharged with so much wounded

45

pride, that there is danger that constructive criticism may be drowned out and the initiative necessary to put things to rights lost in the shuffle. No citizen has to look very far to discover evidence of trouble in our high schools. If he is fortunate enough to find none in his own school he need look no farther than Little Rock or New York, where the mere preservation of law and order has required the occupation of schools by the Army and the police. If these are extreme cases, representing social more than educational problems, they are nonetheless symbolic of cases in many other communities where, amid classrooms crowded to suffocation and double—sometimes triple—sessions, overworked teachers exhaust themselves trying to maintain elementary discipline. Some of this trouble is symptomatic of a teen-age bravado and defiance of authority which, though apparently world-wide in scope, seems to have reached its peak under the auspices of permissive parenthood in the United States. It is symptomatic, too, of teacher shortages, cramped quarters, and lack of essential equipment caused by ignoring our population curve and failing to read its plain educational implications.

Economic reports of these conditions have been given almost continuous publicity, but they have not produced a remedy, for these are not economic phenomena. A nation's schools are part of its culture, and the indifference with which ours have been treated bespeaks a cultural rather than an economic failing. We have always had the money to provide for their needs and provide for them liberally. We have it today. Last year we spent more on tobacco and liquor; more on new and used cars; more on recreation than we spent on our entire system of education, including all our elementary and secondary schools as well as our colleges and universities, public and private. Once the need for more intensive research in intercontinental and space missiles, costly as it is, is borne in upon us, we have little difficulty in providing the funds for it. Our failure to support our schools in similar fashion is fundamentally a failure to see their purpose in our civilization.

Such a failure could lead to disaster. The pages of history are full of instances of the collapse of nations and the decline and disappearance of civilizations that began with cultural decay and were accompanied and hastened by it. Failure of the United States today to live up to the ideals and fulfill the promise of its own civilization could have similar results. We are engaged in something more than a race into space. The prospect is that, although we may soon go voyaging among the planets, we shall have to return from our travels and continue to dwell upon the earth. Our ability to do so successfully—that is to say, more successfully than other animals and civilizations that have become extinct—will depend upon two things. We shall have to produce not only a scientific competence but also a political and a social competence equal to the task. Both of these responsibilities devolve upon our educational system, particularly upon our high schools. Their capacity to discharge them depends, in turn, upon what value we attach to our way of life.

One thing is certain. We shall not achieve the minimum military security essential to the continuance and further development of that way of life unless we improve upon one particular kind of education. This is the kind that culminates in mastery of the basic sciences, the humanities, and the social sciences, that produces through its followers the scientific discoveries upon which our technology is founded and much of our physical welfare and our military security depend—the knowledge and wisdom that shape our laws and social institutions and guide our public policies; the spiritual and aesthetic refinement that bears fruit in our arts. It is from this kind of education that all the major professions—medicine, law, divinity, teaching, the

47

sciences, and increasingly the fine arts and engineering—recruit their apprentices. For it is this kind of education that most fully and effectively develops the ability of the individual to grapple with the difficult tasks demanded by these professions. In increasing measure, too, business and industry are turning to this kind of education for technicians and managerial personnel; and the armed forces, having judged its results in two world wars, have given it a preferred place in their officer-training programs. Thus it is to this kind of education that we must look for the competence that will enable us to survive and, we hope, prosper in the world in which we are fated to live.

In its high school phase this kind of education comprises the subjects already cited in the Russian curriculum, with English substituted for Russian as the native language and literature. The irony is that we should have to learn anything about the virtues of such education from Russia. For this was the education out of which the charters of American freedom emerged, the education of the founding fathers, the model they bequeathed to us. A full century before the U.S.S.R. was ever dreamed of, John Adams and Thomas Jefferson were defining its curriculum, its role in our society, and its relation to our form of government, and advocating it as the equal opportunity of all Americans. Most of the countries of the western world had esteemed this type of education (as they still do) the most vital and fruitful of all, yet limited it (as they still do) to a privileged or highly selected few. The United States set an example to the world by opening it up to all who showed the ability and the desire for it.

This is not the first time the U.S.S.R. has taken a leaf out of our educational book. In 1918 progressive education on the then popular American model became the rule in the same Russian schools that have swung far to the other extreme today. After a trial of sixteen years, this curriculum, at first thought to be the perfect educational counterpart of the revolution and its ideals, was found wanting and summarily abolished. During its heyday educational standards sank so low that Soviet officials finally rebelled. They complained that their children could neither read nor write properly, nor do simple arithmetic accurately, and that they were intellectually undisciplined. The result was a decree that brought the Russian grammar and high school curriculum back into phase with the curriculum of the English public school, the German *Gymnasium*, the French *lycée*, and the academic curriculum of the strongest American public high schools and private college preparatory schools. At the same time it launched an effort that today enrolls in that curriculum a higher proportion of school age children than in any other country, including our own.

The Russians have bitten off a large mouthful. Already there are signs of vocational alternatives—"polytechnization" it is called—creeping into the system, accompanied by the creation of boarding schools, both suggesting limits to the hold of their academic curriculum over so large and undifferentiated a mass of students. Khrushchev has announced a plan the effect if not the aim of which would be to reduce the number of those who prepare for higher education but fail to gain admission to it by diverting a larger proportion of students to vocational training and actual employment after only eight years of school. Whatever the underlying reasons for this plan may be—the needs of the labor force, shortage of space in the universities, or the dawning fear of an absolutist regime of too much general education—the fact is that the scope of the Russian academic curriculum could be considerably curtailed and still represent a more ambitious and more systematic effort to

49

exploit the type of education it embodies in the national and the public interest than we are making, with greater resources and stronger tradition in our favor.

What can we do about it? There is practically no limit to what we can do once we make up our minds it is worth doing. Here is an objective that requires no summit conference with foreign powers, no departure from American tradition, no funds we cannot easily afford and readily provide—in fact, nothing save a clear view of the goal and the courage of our conviction that it must and can be attained. Seldom has an objective as vital to the national interest as this been so surely within our reach.

Unfortunately, most of us get no farther in this direction than damning the schools and waiting for Washington to do something about them. If this attitude prevails, the cause will be lost. Though the federal government can help, it is we ourselves in our local communities who must accomplish our educational salvation. I do not say this for traditional reasons—because it always has been so—but because in the nature of the case I believe it must be so. In our scheme of things, education is almost as much a matter of individual conscience as religion is. This is as true of its institutions as it is of its students. In the final analysis, both achieve their greatest heights because they wish to, not because they are compelled to.

Schools draw their main sustenance, which is intellectual and moral, from the community whose interests they serve; and no matter what outside controls we establish over them, they continue to reflect the character of that community. As an individual may borrow money from his bank and still remain an individual, a community may appeal for and accept federal aid and still remain a community. Many schools could benefit by such aid; many, it would seem, will languish without it. But the aid itself will merely enable the local community to perform a function which only it can perform, a crutch that makes it possible for the patient to get to work, not a substitute to do his work for him. Educational standards may be proposed by Washington. They will be disposed by the local community. Any further progress toward federal direction or control would not only touch an extremely sensitive nerve in our body politic; it would almost certainly fail in its objective. Even in the Soviet educational system, with absolute dictatorial power to enforce uniformity and a population conditioned for centuries to accept it, evidence points to familiar disparities in standards and accomplishments: between urban and rural schools, for example; between schools of different regions, for another example; and between schools reflecting different local customs and attitudes, for still another. It is hard to conceive of any American analogy, however benevolent, however severe, that would either smother or substitute for local initiative in education.

It will help matters, therefore, if we recognize at the outset that we shall have to work toward our goal in a variety of ways appropriate to a great variety of individual situations and circumstances. The large urban school stripped of support by migration to the suburbs will have one problem on its hands. The rural school in need of consolidation with its neighbors will have another. The school amidst city slums will have urgent business of a nature that rarely comes to the attention of the suburban school surrounded by the families of college graduates and attended by their children; and so on. Public school life is the private life of the American people turned inside out, in all its diversity, and is hardly more amenable to centralized authority than it is in the home.

51

Still, we can spend our energies to better effect than damning the schools and waiting for Washington to bail them out of their troubles. Destructive criticism gets us nowhere, and we have had a surfeit of it. And the plain truth is that unless there is a change of heart on the part of the public, federal aid, however necessary, will not bail the schools out of their troubles. On the contrary, it will be more likely to give those troubles a new lease on life. When a bright boy (or girl) who should be taking advanced mathematics elects in its place a course in homemaking so that he can study with his "date," what difference will it make if the waste of talent takes place in a new glass building instead of an old brick one? Or if the teacher or the principal who permitted such a thing to happen has his salary raised? Federal appropriations to either purpose would only amount to a subsidization of error. Before they can do any real good, the public attitude toward education, particularly toward high school education, will have to undergo a serious change.

Consider, for example, a widespread parental attitude toward two fundamental parts of the educational process, namely discipline and homework. Without self-discipline there can be no self-education, and without self-education there can be no education. A student learns self-discipline by learning to measure up to discipline, which in the first instance must be enforced by authority; and the school that does not teach him this fails him badly. Yet our schools are severely limited in the amount and kind of discipline they can administer; and even in this, more often than not, they find parents interceding and conspiring against them. The state of affairs in New York, where recently forty-one schools had to be occupied by the police, seems hardly more than the logical conclusion to such an attitude. Certainly it will improve the schools' chances of keeping order in the classroom to relieve overcrowding through new construction, and to employ more teachers. But until parents generally take a different view of the matter the results are not likely to be commensurate with the investment.

With respect to homework, the attitude of parents often presents an even greater handicap to the educational process. Any student attempting to cross the bridge of high-school-into-college education should be carrying five solid academic courses, and to do justice to these should be doing fifteen to twenty uninterrupted hours of homework a week. Yet I have heard more than one harried teacher complain that such assignments only bring parental intercession; and I have heard principals groan in despair at the same thing. It is hard to understand how anyone can believe in learning without studying. Perhaps it comes from the contemplation of denicotined tobacco, decalorized desserts, or any of the innumerable ways the advertising industry has devised for us to have something for nothing, satisfaction without effort, a gay dance without paying the piper. Or could it be the attitude that seeks greater economic rewards for less work applied in false analogy to education? Whatever it is, it diminishes the educational opportunity of *all* students, not just the gifted; it does great injustice to parents who understand the reason for discipline and homework and actively support the schools in their efforts to maintain both; it costs the schools, their teachers, and their students huge losses in time, money, and effort, and it represents another poor risk for federal funds.

Yet another parental attitude that bedevils our high schools is the one that gives the entertainment of spectators of athletic sports priority over the educational needs of their participants. We have seen the excesses to which this attitude could go in higher education, where, at least in some quarters, the tide appears to have turned. It would not be amiss for us to give some thought to its effects upon secondary education. I have heard of actual cases of consolidations of struggling high schools, below the optimum in size and strapped for teachers, being obstructed by adult followers of the local basketball teams. And I have heard superintendents and principals give vent to the same despairing sentiments at the inroads of the spectator interest in football as have my colleagues in the universities. Few of the latter question the validity of amateur athletics as an integral part of the educational process, nor do I. But I do question whether the entertainment business is; and if I were responsible for the administration of federal funds, I should want a strict accounting in this regard.

Having introduced a theme primarily affecting men, I now touch upon one of particular concern to women. Persons knowledgeable in such matters inform me that in the election by competent students of easy nonacademic in place of more difficult academic courses, girls are worse offenders than boys. The fact seems surprising, for at that age girls are more intellectually mature than boys and are on the average more proficient in academic studies. Why then do they shy away from them?

I suggest two reasons. One is the belief that a course in cooking or marriage-and-the-family will produce, later on, a better home and a happier life than, say, a course in English literature or mathematics. The other is that women, having gained access to higher education, seem not to have gained complete confidence in its fulfillment. Both reasons discount the importance to the country as well as to the individual of the careers open to college-trained women —particularly in teaching, where, in the existing teacher shortage, their services are at a premium. Both overlook the vital role that could be played by every mother in the educational life of her children, in directing their energies, supervising their studies, and, beyond and above all, inculcating in them a respect for education and the motive to make the most of it. American education has no greater stake in any of its sources of support than this. It is largely to the mother of the family that it must look for proper attitudes toward discipline and homework, and for cooperation in many other respects. She is the school's partner in the educational enterprise, often the more important and influential partner of the two; and the better her education, the better the education of her children will be, and the better the school. Every girl who has the competence for a solid academic course and spends it on a pleasing or seemingly "practical" nonacademic substitute commits at least as great a waste—often a greater—of as much consequence to society, as any boy.

It should be clear by now that the underlying premise to the theory of high school education as a bridge to college education is that it be used as such. It is true that we expect other duties of our high schools of great importance to society. Sometimes it seems as though there were few responsibilities for our teen-age citizens that we have not delegated to them. By school attendance laws, child labor laws, and labor union practices, we have systematically excluded this age group from the labor market. We have little room or time for them in our homes. We have turned them over to the schools and asked these to bring them up for us. Not all these children are qualified for higher education or even for the academic curriculum leading up to it. Yet they are required by law to remain in school and receive instruction of some sort. For these, alternatives to the academic curriculum are in order, and it is obviously in the national interest that such nonacademic, vocational programs be brought up to as high a standard as obtains in Russia or anywhere else, and that funds, facilities, and teachers be provided for that purpose. Yet if we are to achieve our main objective, the primary concern of the high school must be its academic curriculum.

The two aims are not incompatible, but they are distinct. Yet as things stand now, their distinctness is not as clear as it should be, and no wonder. They have become confused in a plethora of courses of all kinds and descriptions which have grown in number from around 35 in 1910 to over 300 by 1950. In the process, many have undergone protean changes, as history has into social studies; English into journalism and radio broadcasting; algebra into general mathematics; physics and chemistry into general science. Meanwhile, home economics has spawned such a numerous progeny that it defies description, with nonvocational industrial arts; vocational trade and industrial arts; business education; health, safety, and physical education; music; art; and numerous other programs rivaling it in fecundity. The proportion of students enrolled in these curriculums is large and would be larger if all nonacademic course elections by academic students were taken into account. For the elective system that once ran riot in college education now brings an equal freedom of curricular choice to students in high school education, and at a time when they are relatively less competent to exercise it.

Many make this choice, or have it made for them, on a basis that fails to do justice either to their own native ability or to the merits of the academic curriculum. For example, it is widely assumed that the vocational curriculums are better suited to students who are not going on to college than is the academic curriculum. This assumption rests upon two premises, both open to serious doubt. The first is that the academic curriculum is less valuable to students for whom high school is the final educational experience than it is to those for whom it is the preparation for higher

56

education. If the academic curriculum possesses the virtues I have claimed for it, it could well be argued that it is more, rather than less, important to those for whom high school represents the last chance at it. The second dubious premise is that present methods of testing and guidance according to which students are separated and enrolled in the two curriculums are entirely reliable. The results suggest that they are not entirely reliable, that there is a wide margin of error and waste in which the academic curriculum might prove itself. My own conviction is that both vocational and academic curriculums are necessary, but that the academic curriculum has never been given the chance it deserves of our high school students or they deserve of it.

It is a wary student who can pick his way without stumbling or side-stepping through such a thicket. Parental guidance could help him, provided, as already suggested, such guidance is itself informed by higher education. Aptitude tests can help him, but at age 13 or 14 aptitude is not always fully revealed. Nor can aptitude tests guarantee motive; and what good is aptitude without motive? In the Soviet Union this student would be prodded and coerced by sanctions which are completely out of the question with us, whatever results they may or may not ultimately yield in Russia. In short, apart from his own judgment, which at age 13 or 14 is yet but half formed, the American high school candidate for the academic curriculum leading to higher education is dependent upon his teachers. It is they who will have to help him discover himself. If they see the bridge clearly and see it whole, the chances are he will negotiate it. If they do not see it thus, the chances are he will not.

My final suggestion is, therefore, that we give fresh thought to our teacher-training programs with a view to strengthening them in the subjects of the academic curriculum. I do not think there is any more crucial point at which the whole problem we have been discussing could be attacked than this. Generally speaking, these programs are replete with courses in methodology which I believe equip the prospective teacher less well than courses in the subject matter he is preparing to teach, combined with the actual experience of teaching, properly supervised, in practice and apprenticeship. Again, if students are to be sorted out according to the distinct aims of the vocational and the academic curriculums, so, I think, should teachers be. Mastery of one or more of the basic subjects in the academic curriculum is a full-time career, as anyone who has attempted it can testify. It is such mastery that gives the teacher his main—indeed, his only real—authority over his students. Every effort should be made to prepare him for the conditions he will encounter in his classroom by anticipating them in practice and apprentice teaching, and by analyzing and interpreting this experience while it is still fresh. But the teacher's most reliable weapon for keeping order in the classroom, and by far his most reliable instrument for discovering candidates for higher education and getting them across the bridge, will be his command of the subject he teaches.

Education, it has often been said, should form a continuity, even a unity, in the life of the individual who experiences it, interrupted only by the physical separation of the institutions he attends. To complete the unity of the academic curriculum we should include its teachers in it as well as their students. Teachers reared in this tradition will be the best hope, too, of educating the public whose attitude is so largely responsible for the present state of affairs.

Money will be needed for all these things. Teachers'

salaries will have to be improved, buildings built, necessary equipment installed. But something is needed to supply the money. Not that we do not have it; we have enough and to spare. What is needed is the purpose to spend it on our schools. The Russians have shocked us into an awareness of our educational ills. But shock treatment alone will not cure these. The real cure lies in discovering the place of education in American society that the founders of that society intended for it.

Although the process of discovery has begun, to complete it will not be easy for us. There are so many things to spend our money on other than education, more things than ever existed in any country in the world. If we are to find the rightful place for education amidst all these, we shall have to seek it as Bunyan's pilgrims sought the way to the Celestial City through the teeming alleys of Vanity Fair. There they found "houses, lands, trades, places, honours, preferments, titles, countries, kingdoms, lusts, pleasures, and delights of all sorts" for sale; and they were inveigled by "jugglers, cheats, games, plays, fools, apes, and rogues, and that of every kind." All the arts of salesmanship were concentrated upon them, but to no avail. And when the baffled hawkers asked them, "What will ye buy?" the pilgrims replied, "We buy the truth."

On Reading

If ever coals were brought to Newcastle I bring them with these words to the literary profession. What can I say to the writers, publishers, booksellers, printers, and critics of books whose collected works are called the true universities? I read my fate in the diary of James Hadley, Professor of Greek in Yale College from 1854 to 1872 and father of President Hadley. Returning from a faculty meeting in the year 1852, he foretells my present circumstances as follows:

> The state of things at Western Reserve College is really deplorable, and the case of Mr. Pierce, their President, is in some respects a hard one. They have kept him begging for 6 years or more, and now complain that he is fit for nothing else. Mr. Olmsted having said something about the attempts of alumni in Amherst and Williams to dictate in regard to College matters, Mr. Woolsey said, "Mark my prediction: if our alumni meet together year after year, with nothing to do but talk, and time enough for that, they will be trying to govern us. You must shut their mouths with long addresses."

My case, too, is a hard one. Begging and—shall we say medium length—addresses and the intricacies of "academical superintendence" have removed me from your company which I once greatly cherished, removed me so far that I am safe even from guilt by association, broken me through the ranks from writer to reader, all the way back to general reader, private first class. Gone are the orgies of reading that began, for me, with *Leatherstocking Tales* and *Froissart's Chronicle*, that continued, albeit, under competition, through school and college, and that became standard fare in graduate school and teaching days. All I have been able to salvage is the habit of reading myself to sleep every night. I have kept this same habit (and by skillful use of spotlights and sleepshades, the same wife) for nearly twenty-five years. In, on, and under our bedside table is a motley library for every mood. It includes at the moment, Shakespeare, Shaw, Plutarch, Joseph Swain's *Ancient World*, Francis Biddle's *Fear of Freedom*, United States Reports Vol. 341 (containing the Supreme Court's opinions affirming the conviction of the Communist party officials), Roland H. Bainton's *Travail of Religious Liberty*, Elliot Paul's *Black Gardenia*, A. P. Herbert's *Number Nine or the Mind Sweepers,* Volumes 2 and 3 of the Princeton University Press edition of *The Papers of Thomas Jefferson,* the Treasurer's Report of Yale University (in case of late calls from alumni) , and the New Testament. It is a wonderful pharmacopoeia, more potent than sleeping pills when I wish to sleep or coffee when I wish to stay awake. It is the consolation of my academical superintendence. It is all I have to justify my claim to address you as anything but a technological illiterate.

My narrow escape from technological illiteracy—if indeed it prove to be an escape and not just temporary immunity—causes me to ponder the fate of our country, in which this disease is endemic and is spreading like the elm blight. What happens when we are all too busy to read, when our ways of life and work combined with the substitutes for reading now in mass production and use finally conquer our taste for reading as well as our belief in its utility? I know—my own metaphor implies it—that you can drug yourself with reading. I know that there are sermons in stones and books in the running brooks. As a teacher of young men for nearly a quarter century, I have been unusually sensitive to their elders' appeals to experience and action. Ours is an age of action, hair-trigger action, and we cannot resign from it. But what is to become of us when action no longer finds inspiration or discipline in thought because thought has not been able to find inspiration or discipline in books?

Is the question rhetorical? I do not think so. There was a day in the history of this republic when its men of affairs found time to read and demonstrated, in their own lives and works, the utility as well as the delight of reading. The four master builders, Hamilton, John Adams, Jefferson, and Madison, were probably the four most widely read men of their age. Certainly this was true of Adams, Jefferson, and Madison, and it might have been true of the impetuous Hamilton had he survived his impetuosity. For we find him at eighteen as an undergraduate student as deep in the classics of law and philosophy as his more studious collaborator on *The Federalist* of a decade later.

Our prize-winning poet, Miss Moore, says of poetic images, "these things are important not because . . . a high-sounding interpretation can be put upon them but because they are useful." Never, to my knowledge, did men find more practical and more immediate use in reading than these four. Between them, though they were in politics all their lives, in an age of intermittent war and revolution, serving as congressional delegates, ambassadors, governors, constitution makers, cabinet members and presidents, they read virtually every book in print in the western world. And out of all this reading? It had very little application to any particular views, says Adams somewhat disingenuously of his own case,

> till these debates in Congress and the interrogatories in public and private, turned my thoughts to these researches, which produced the *Thoughts on Government*, the Constitution of Massachusetts, and at length the *Defence of the Constitutions of the United States*, and the *Discourses on Davila*, writings which have never done any good to me, though some of them undoubtedly contributed to produce the Constitution of New York, the Constitution of the U.S., and the last Constitutions of Pennsylvania and Georgia. They undoubtedly, also, contributed to the writings of Publius, called the Federalist, which were all written after the publication of my work in Philadelphia, New York, and Boston.

The reading lists of Jefferson and Madison and the historical accomplishments of the four men establish beyond cavil the general validity of Adams' claim. Do you know these lists? Let me cite Jefferson's education for a lawyer. "Till eight o'clock in the morning"—not *from* eight but *till* eight—he prescribes the reading of books on physical studies, ethics, religion, and natural law; from eight to twelve, law; from twelve to one, politics and political economy; in the afternoon, history; and "From Dark to Bedtime," belles lettres, criticism, rhetoric and oratory. Each subject is subdivided categorically and ballasted by scores of titles, all of which Jefferson had read himself. His Literary Bible and Commonplace Book expand this list, as do his letters, particularly those to his nephew Peter Carr, until, as I have said, it includes virtually every book in print in the western world.

This was no bibliolatry. It was the earnest, inner, creative life of a man who taught himself at least three ancient and four modern foreign languages so that he might pursue the uses of reading to their ultimate limits. Out of this life, which he shared most intimately with Adams and Madison, came the charters of American democracy: the Declaration of Independence, the state constitutions with their bills of rights; the federal Constitution with its Bill of Rights; the Bill for the More General Diffusion of Knowledge and the Bill for Establishing Religious Freedom in Virginia; the public documents and state papers embedded in a matrix of private correspondence which the three men kept up to within a few days of their deaths (and they all outlived the biblical span), Jefferson in a hand painfully crippled by a broken wrist, Adams till his hand and wrist became so weak from old age that he had to dictate to his niece; a body of writing which in Jefferson's case, in the definitive edition now in preparation at Princeton, is expected to fill over fifty volumes, and to which again in Jefferson's case, Abraham Lincoln, another great reader, said he turned whenever he wished to refer to the "definitions and axioms of free society."

So much for the uses of reading in that age. What of our own age, in which war and revolution are putting those definitions and axioms to the severest test they have endured since birth? In Washington, I learn, a university is about to open a course for ghost writers, who "will be taught to write in such a way that orators will understand at all times what they are saying." Ghost writers are "indispensable artisans," an official of the university declares. There are "more than 150 of them on the top level in Washington alone. Most of the great speeches we hear are written in whole or in part by someone backstage." The writers of these speeches have a hard time adjusting their talents "to fit the mental and oratorical capacities" of the men for whom they are writing. Hence the course. What advice and counsel could these indispensable artisans obtain from Jefferson? Suppose, by chance, they turned to his letter to Peter Carr in 1785, when Jefferson was ambassador to France and his nephew was just entering upon his serious studies:

> It is time for you now to begin to be choice in your reading . . . I advise you to begin a course of ancient history, reading everything in the original and not in translation. First read Goldsmith's history of Greece. This will give you a digested view of that field. Then take up ancient history in the detail, reading the following books, in the following order: Herodotus, Thucydides, Xenophontis Anabasis, Arrian, Quintus Curtius, Diodorus Siculus, Justin. This shall form the first stage of your historical reading, and is all I need mention to you now. The next will be of Roman history (Livy, Sallust, Caesar, Cicero's epistles, Suetonius, Tacitus, Gibbon) . In Greek and Latin poetry you . . . will read . . . Virgil, Terence, Horace, Anacreon, Theocritus, Homer, Euripides, Sophocles. Read also Milton . . . Shakespeare, Ossian, Pope's and Swift's works, in order to form your style in your own language. In morality, read Epictetus, Xenophontis Memorabilia, Plato's Socratic dialogues, Cicero's philosophies, Antoninus and Seneca.

What would our ghost writers say to this? The very reading of the words puts a hex on their profession.

"Reading," in Bacon's aphorism, "maketh a full man, conference a ready man, and writing an exact man." What are we doing under our forest of television masts, with our indispensable artisans the ghost writers, our analysts, opin-

65

ion samplers, and committees of brainpickers? We are succumbing one by one to technological illiteracy. We have traded in the mind's eye for the eye's mind. We are conferring. We have not quite given up reading. Here and there, in a few homes, in a few educational institutions, it still hangs on in competition with more efficient methods and processes, such as the extrasensory and the audiovisual. A few teachers still prefer written essays to intellectual bingo games that can be scored by electricity. A few students still like to read, a few statesmen, I suppose, still carry books with them when they travel. I am still reading in bed, and you who write and publish the books I read are still earning a modest competence.

But what if present trends continue? Since reading maketh us full men, when we stop reading we shall be empty men. Since men who do not read have no use for writing, and in any case empty men have nothing to write about, we shall stop writing. We shall then be empty and inexact, though presumably we shall still be able to confer and conference will still make us ready. Ready for what? For some technological *deus ex machina* to finish the plot we have forgotten how to write? For some graduate of the school for ghost writers to whisper to us from the prompter's box?

They will not serve us. They cannot promote the more general diffusion of knowledge essential to a democratic society because they are mere transmitters; they cannot inform the statesmen to whom that society must look for the preservation and renewal of its charters because they are themselves uninformed. During the past century the average working week of our industrial and white collar workers has shrunk from seventy to less than forty hours. The millions of man hours thus conserved form the new Colossus. This Colossus has more leisure at his disposal than all the aristocracies of history, all the patrons of art, all the captains of industry and kings of enterprise. What will he do with it? Will he read? Will he make himself a full man and an exact man, or will he be content to be merely a ready man—a measure of muscle and a shout from the mob? The choice lies before him. Who will help him make it?

Fellow citizens of the world of books, as an academical superintendent I make common cause with you. I hope *we* will!

On Conversation

Conversation in this country has fallen upon evil days. The great creative art whereby man translates feeling into reason and shares with his fellow man those innermost thoughts and ideals of which civilization is made is beset by forces which threaten its demise. It is forsaken by a technology that is so busy tending its time-saving devices that it has no time for anything else. It is drowned out in singing commercials by the world's most productive economy that has so little to say for itself it has to hum it. It is hushed and shushed in dimly lighted parlors by television audiences who used to read, argue, and even play bridge, an old-fashioned card game requiring speech. It is shouted down by devil's advocates, thrown into disorder by points of order. It is subdued by soft-voiced censors who, in the name of public relations, counsel discretion and the avoidance of controversy, like so many family physicians breaking the news gently and advising their patients to cut down on their calories. It starves for want of reading and reflection. It languishes in a society that spends so much time passively listening and being talked to that it has all but lost the will and the skill to speak for itself.

I wonder how many of us are aware of this predicament and interested in its possible consequences. It was conversation, reaching its orderly and exalted climax in the dialogues of Socrates, which, in an age without books or their latter-day substitutes, laid the foundations of the civilization we are dedicated to defend. It was conversation of which the New Testament, the greatest teaching ever recorded, was composed. It was conversation, among small groups of university scholars still in a bookless world that revived learning at the end of the Dark Ages. "I am a great believer in conversation," said Whitehead toward the end of his life. "Outside of the book-knowledge which is necessary to our professional training, I think I have got most of my development from the good conversation to which I have always had the luck to have access." Conversation is the oldest form of instruction of the human race. It is still an indispensable one. Great books, scientific discoveries, works of art, great perceptions of truth and beauty in any form—all require great conversation to complete their meaning: without it they are abracadabra—color to the blind or music to the deaf. Conversation, inventing its own substitute for words, has accomplished the greatest miracle known to pedagogy in piercing the veil that hung between the infant Helen Keller and nothingness and bringing her into mature objective knowledge of the world after a normal subjective experience of it of only nineteen months. Conversation is the handmaid of learning, true religion, and free government. It would be impossible to put too high a price on all we stand to lose by suffering its decay.

How then do we account for the symptoms of decadence? Are they the result of a sinister softening-up process such as preceded the dictators of recent history not to mention Big Brother of 1984? Or are they our own fault? Are we being softened up or are we merely softening? In either case, what can we do about it? I think that the present predicament of conversation in America is our own fault, and I take courage from the thought. For what is our fault lies within our power to correct. I think there are a number of things we can do about it, and I propose to suggest a few that ought to be encouraged and capitalized for the benefit of the nation.

Let me first defend the thesis that the predicament from which we suffer is our own fault and not something slipped over on us by conspiracy. Consider all the tools and toys of our prolific economy—the time-saving, labor-saving devices, the automatic cookers and washers, the almost automatic automobile that will present us with a new industrial tautology when it becomes complete, the 3-D movies and the television sets. Do these distract us from conversation any more than the toil and drudgery they have supplanted? Perhaps not, but that is not the point. The point is that they have given us more leisure than the human race has ever known and in more equal, democratic measure; yet instead of making that leisure the ally of conversation we seem content with it as no less of a distraction than drudgery. Is this the result of machination or conspiracy? I find it hard to believe so. I find it much easier to believe that it is nobody's fault but our own, and I rest my case on a cardinal principle of American business. This principle is, the customer is always right. If he wants fatter, more expensive cars, he shall have them. If he wants bubble gum and comics, he shall have them too. And if he wants to spend his time looking and listening without ever discussing with his friends the meaning of what he sees and hears, that too is his prerogative. We look in vain for scapegoats in this quarter. The trouble here is toys, not traitors.

I would argue the same of scapegoats in general. Orderly conversation in its parliamentary sphere, the sphere essential to free government, has been much abused and disrupted of late, and the abuses and disruptions have spread like ripples from a stone cast into a pond, stirring up strife all over the country. The effect of this strife has been to inhibit conversation and make a case for the public relations experts; and some critics have found individuals responsible for the phenomenon. I do not agree with them. On the contrary, I think we are responsible for the individuals. I think we are responsible because we, the people, elected and appointed such individuals to represent us, and that is exactly what they are doing. They are representing our fears and suspicions.

This, I think, constitutes a real peril to the country, but not of the kind commonly deplored by the critics of such individuals. Bacon told us long ago that believing a rumor was as bad as starting a rumor. He said,

> Suspicions amongst thoughts are like bats among birds, they ever fly by twilight. Certainly they are to be repressed, or at least well guarded, for they cloud the mind; they leese [lose] friends; and they check [interfere] with business, whereby business cannot go on currently and constantly. They dispose Kings to tyranny, husbands to jealousy, wise men to irresolution and melancholy. They are defects not in the heart but in the brain . . . There is nothing makes a man suspect much, more than to know little; and therefore men should remedy suspicion by procuring to know more . . .

Suspicions arouse passions. If we become creatures of passion the individuals who represent us will represent passion. The danger is not that one or another of them may attempt to make himself dictator: I have enough faith in this country to believe that such an attempt would inevitably fail, all European analogies to the contrary notwithstanding. The danger is that we ourselves allow passion to blind us to things we should see with clear eyes and calculate with cool heads and so lead us to a Pearl Harbor compounded of hydrogen. In either case—the hypothetical one of a foreign-style *coup d'état* or the imminent danger that passions may cloud our minds, interfere with our business, and so bring us to disaster—the remedy is "procuring to know more" ourselves, not hunting scapegoats to blame for our own shortcomings.

By this path I came to our universities and the extraordinary opportunity open to them. Can you think of a better place for "procuring to know more" or for conversation to prove itself as a means to that end? Where else save Elysium itself is life so congenial to this combination as it is in a university, particularly a residential university? Where else does conversation play so vital a part in the central purpose of the institution? Where else, though hard pressed from without, does it yet survive so stubbornly and hold out so much hope to those who would encourage it? Whitehead is but the most distinguished of educational philosophers, most of whom appear to us in the more familiar context of alumni reunions, to testify to its value in his own education. Our civilization and our sacred liberties can be offered as potential evidence of its value to ours.

How, then, shall we make the most of it? Shall we have courses in conversation? Perish the thought. Let us have, instead, conversation in courses. By conversation in courses, moreover, I do not mean whispering at lectures. I mean as much give and take between teacher and student as is possible in this day of soaring enrollments, teacher shortages, and financial deficits. Let us not forget that there is a point in relation to these seemingly ineluctable limits beyond which teaching becomes mass production and the law of diminishing returns sets in. At its best, teaching is a two-way process, an exchange of thought between teacher and student, by which both profit and the thought exchanged becomes ennobled in the transfer. I do not see how we can make very great compromises with this principle without dashing our hopes for conversation and for higher education as well.

This is a hard row to hoe and we must have help with it. To maintain the proper ratio of teachers to students necessary to avoid such compromises will tax our resources to the utmost; it may well overtax them. Where then shall we look for help? Where better than to our own students imbued with Whitehead's respect for conversation as an educational process, with a sense of its value to the world into which they will graduate, and with the heaven-sent opportunities of cultivating and putting it to use afforded them in college? Here is potential relief from the teacher shortage that would cost nothing, that is present in every liberal arts college worthy of the name, and that needs only to be galvanized to prove its value. I say galvanized, not organized. Organization would kill it. Self-conscious circles of undergraduate pedagogues would, I predict, become ever-decreasing and concentric in character. But undergraduates who resisted the distractions of their elders and, in their own time and place, gave themselves over to conversation that tested and distilled into wisdom the knowledge derived from lectures and books would do honor to the disciples of Socrates and give our universities and our civilization a new lease on life.

To some extent this is already happening. Yet in relation to capacity the reserves of power have scarcely been tapped. They should be. Here is the strength of the residential liberal arts college waiting to be called upon, the principle of self-education waiting to be demonstrated. Both liberal education and the residential college were founded upon that principle, the liberal arts to train men and women to think for themselves, to learn by themselves, to go on educating themselves for the rest of their lives; the residential college to initiate and foster that process not as a club or hotel but as a corporate society of teachers and scholars. Only part of the process can be accomplished through formal instruction. The other, and not always the lesser, part is accomplished in the social life and intercourse of students outside the classroom.

British educators have made much of these principles— the liberal arts and the residential—as they are reflected in the remarkable systems of adult education developed in the Scandinavian countries, especially Denmark, which have served as models to proponents of adult education in Britain since the war. They say, in effect, that they would rather have a group of adult students living together as a residential community for two weeks than they would individually attending night school or taking correspondence courses for two years; and they have carried their convictions into Western Germany. There, for example, one finds in the Collegium Academicum of Heidelberg a conscious (and, so far, apparently successful) attempt to foster the residential principle in a national system of higher education which, like most continental systems, has been almost wholly nonresidential. I cite these cases to show that in the judgment of a people whose educational experience goes back nearly eight hundred years and from whose universities our own are lineal descendants, the residential principle is neither a whim nor a luxury but a vital necessity.

This is in keeping with the character of the American liberal arts college. All any such college needs to do to realize the educational potential I have suggested for it is to live up to that character. With its predominantly residential system of higher education, the United States is favored beyond any other nation in having ready to hand the very means which others emulate and strive to develop with scant resources. Our undergraduate students do not know their own strength. They do not realize the educational benefits they might confer upon all of us and themselves in the bargain by refinement and more extensive practice of the art of conversation.

The forms such conversation should take and the rules it should follow are of course important. Like all art it cannot be formless and it must show obedience to certain classic principles. Jargon is not conversation. Plain English, the purer the better, is essential. One of the things that made possible the attainments of Greek philosophy was the extraordinary fluidity of the Greek language, which the philosophers who are still read used in its purity and never in adulteration. Small talk and gossip are not conversation. Neither is indictment, with which I include any and all one-way processes of insinuation, invective, diatribe, denunciation, excoriation, anathema, and so on, notwithstanding their current popularity. Conversation is an exchange of thought that leaves all parties to it a grain the wiser. It implies progress. Though it may begin anywhere, even in the realm of trivia, it should try to get somewhere and carry everyone with it as it goes.

The basic principles of conversation were established by Socrates both by example and by precept more than two thousand years ago. One of the most important of these was that conversation should take place among friends, in a congenial atmosphere, with common interests at heart. Best of all would be one common interest, namely wisdom. It is interesting to see how these principles anticipate the nature and purpose of our liberal arts colleges. Wisdom, to Socrates, was "the one true coin for which all things ought to be exchanged . . . and only in exchange for this, and in company with this, is anything truly bought or sold, whether courage or temperance or justice. And is not

75

all true virtue the companion of wisdom, no matter what fears or pleasures or other similar goods or evils may or may not attend her?" Such were his last words to his disciples just before he drank the hemlock. Again, in an earlier dialogue, Socrates declares:

> Some things I have said of which I am not altogether confident. But that we shall be better and braver and less helpless if we think that we ought to enquire, than we should have been if we indulged in the idle fancy that there was no knowing and no use in seeking to know what we do not know;—that is a theme upon which I am ready to fight, in word and deed, to the utmost of my power.

Where could we find a better motto for higher education? These are, it is true, the utterances of a consecrated teacher and philosopher rather than merely a gifted conversationalist. Yet they tell us much about both learning and conversation. If Carlyle could define a university as a collection of books, Socrates might well have defined it as a conversation about wisdom. In any event we may conclude from what he did say that conversation about wisdom is true conversation.

To facilitate conversation of this kind, to keep it moving and make it truly productive, Socrates established one practical rule that has served both conversation and learning well ever since. This was his separation of the hypothesis and its consequences into two distinct questions. The hypothesis was first assumed as true. Then the consequences of the hypothesis were deduced, those which agreed with it being accepted as true and those which disagreed rejected as false. The hypothesis was never taken as axiomatic or self-evident and if called into question was debated in its turn. By this method the parties to a conversation were brought onto common ground, unity and relevance were ensured for their discussion, and the whole range of human knowledge was infinitely expanded. What a boon it might be to our troubled world that wastes so much time and temper arguing at cross purposes if we could apply this rule more generally to the discussion of human affairs today. Criticism would have to be answered on its merits rather than by attacks on the critic. Concealed or unstated premises would be brought out into the open. It might even become possible to discuss our foreign policy without raising our voices and accusing one another of treason. Who knows what enlightened dispensations in the national interest might not result? But I am afraid that for such exalted conversation as this we should either have to bring Socrates back to earth or wait as he did in the conviction that the ideals of men were laid away in heaven.

Even supposing we did bring him back to earth and summoned his thought to the matter at hand—the revival of conversation among students in residential colleges of the liberal arts—he might not find the going so easy at first, particularly at this season of the year. I can see him now returning, not from the army at Potidaea or a religious procession at the Piraeus, but, let us say, from a meeting of the Association of Colleges in New England, where he had been demonstrating the impossibility of computing the essential worth of each member institution on four pieces of paper eight and one-half inches wide by eleven inches long. On the train he has encountered graduates of two of the member institutions whose names, with apologies to Owen Johnson and J. P. Marquand, are Dink Stover and Bojo Brown. They engage Socrates in a discussion of education and arrive with dispatch at the following proposition:

77

BOJO: I don't like this new Ivy League Agreement.

DINK: Neither do I. All this business about spring practice and recruiting players!

SOCRATES: Players? What is the Ivy League, a group of actors?

BOJO: No, a group of colleges.

SOCRATES: Ah, and they have just agreed to recruit actors?

DINK: No, they have just agreed not to recruit football players.

SOCRATES: But why should they wish to recruit football players? I thought colleges were for students. At first I thought you were talking about players in the sense of actors or possibly musicians, who would entertain the students and recreate them after their studies. But why football players?

DINK: You tell him, Bojo.

BOJO: Well, you see, a lot of colleges award football scholarships—

SOCRATES: But what has football got to do with scholarship?

BOJO: Well, I see what you mean, but that's what they call them.

SOCRATES: That may be what they call them, but what are they?

DINK (interrupting): They're grants of financial assistance . . .

SOCRATES: Financial assistance? You mean money? You mean young men are paid money to play football in college?

BOJO: In some cases yes, but not in the Ivy League. Although by the way, Dink, a friend of mine in Greenwich told me the other day . . . of course I don't believe it, but I thought you ought to know it's going the rounds, that a Princeton man in his office told him that he knew for a fact that a group of your alumni had offered . . .

DINK: I deny that! And anyway, what about that fellow up in Buffalo who was registered in our freshman class and then a group of your alumni grabbed him as he was stepping off the train and . . .

BOJO: Oh, that old chestnut! I . . .

SOCRATES: Gentlemen, all this talk about football and chestnuts! I thought we were discussing education.

DINK and BOJO, testily, and in unison: WE ARE!

Even with the help of Socrates we should have work to do before the art of conversation in our colleges came into its own. We should have to ensure our students a proper subject of conversation. Fortunately we have this, too, ready to hand in our liberal arts curriculum. This is the educational birthright of undergraduates. Its currency has never been devalued: it is still at par with the currency of Socrates' one true coin. With its perceptions of greatness and excellence, its intimations of immortality, it embodies the full meaning the Greeks gave to virtue and Socrates himself gave to wisdom. As a source of great conversation it has never been equaled. I do not decry vocational training. In some form or other it is essential for most of us and has something to offer all of us. What I do decry is vocational training masquerading as liberal education and usurping its place. The demand of society for the immediate and the utilitarian is unremitting. The Sophists answered it in Socrates' day. What if Socrates had followed suit?

Education can always cash in on this demand. I sometimes ask myself what might have happened if my own university had started cashing in on it when it was first felt. Let us take the timely case of television. It is said to be revolutionizing American life and we are urged to introduce courses in it in our curriculum. There have been several such inventions that were thought by contemporaries to be revolutionary agents of change in American life. The first was the telegraph, whose inventor and his associates, as I recall it, were so awe-struck by their handiwork that their first signaled message was "What hath God wrought!" Next came the telephone, then movies, then radio, and finally TV. Each one of these inventions, speedily put into mass production and consumption, was fraught with no less revolutionary consequences for our society and accompanied by no less apocalyptic prophecies than those which accompany television today.

Suppose, in view of this, Yale had added courses in the techniques and uses of each to its liberal arts curriculum. I can imagine an entering freshman with the course of study catalogue in his hand. He finds courses in telegraphy, telephony, cinematography, radiotelegraphy and telephony, and—words fail me to describe the science of television. Then come the influence courses, the influence of the telegraph on the telephone, the influence of the telephone on radio, the influence of radio on the movies, and so on. Then the influence of influence courses, e.g. the influence of radio and telephonic techniques on communication and its impact on the American family. The freshman reads on in despair. He is looking for a course in English. He can't find one. He goes to the Dean. "English?" says the Dean. "Oh we don't bother with that any more. We have developed more effective means of communication."

The most important thing about any form of communication is what is communicated. The most important thing about what is communicated is its valuation in the currency of Socrates' coin. The utilitarian skills and techniques of each generation are soon outmoded. The search for wisdom and virtue never is. Not all the technological triumphs of history have satisfied man's need for these, nor displaced or even approached them as the most inspiring and fruitful of all subjects of human conversation.

We must manage to present this subject to our undergraduates in such a way as will inspire them to help revive conversation in this tongue-tied democracy that has such good ideas yet cannot speak its own mind.

The Fine Arts and
the University

Half a century ago it would have been hard to talk about the place of the fine arts in a university without begging the question. A few institutions of higher learning maintained schools or departments of architecture, painting, and music, but these enjoyed hardly more than squatters' rights among their venerable academic neighbors. They had little or no support from a public whose taste in art was as uncouth as it was untutored and whose attitude toward those who pursued artistic careers was a mixture of misspent puritanism and unspent philistinism. Within the universities, the fine arts were kept at arm's length by an educational philosophy that refused to recognize them as of equal or even comparable value to studies based upon language, literature, and the sciences. Even among devotees of art feelings were mixed, with many, probably most, practicing artists scornful of its small band of academic champions.

Today the curtain rises on a very different scene. Millions of school children busy themselves with painting and music, and thousands of young men and women go on to college and carry on their pursuit of art with ardor and academic credit thrown into the bargain. In the universities they find architecture, painting, sculpture, the graphic arts, music, and drama competing for their interest more vigorously and with greater success than some of the subjects once held in higher academic esteem.

To be sure, there are still professors who look upon their artistic colleagues as poachers, and artists who regard universities as stiflers of art. But the number of creative artists who, during the past two decades, have found congenial homes in our colleges and universities gives assurance that mutual antipathies have yielded to feelings of mutual affinity and that both sides have accepted university effort in this field as a *fait accompli*. Paul Hindemith, Douglas Moore, Quincy Porter, Robert Frost, Archibald MacLeish, Robert Penn Warren, Mary Ellen Chase, Walter Gropius, and Josef Albers are but a few of those artists who have not merely visited universities for a term or two but have lived and worked in them for long periods of their productive careers, discovering in them new scope for their talents, new opportunities for the training of their apprentices and the artistic education of their audiences. The fine arts have won a place in the academic sun.

The rise of the fine arts in the universities has paralleled their rise in the nation to the highest and most promising stage of their development. May we not expect the momentum to continue? We may if we understand what gives that momentum its initial impetus. Many forces contributed to the rise of the fine arts in the United States. The greater ease of foreign travel, the efforts of collectors and patrons, radio, the coming of age of American civilization—not to mention the inherent power of great art to plead its own case—must all be reckoned among those forces along with higher education. If the universities are to further the progress of the arts they must do more than provide hospitality to artists in residence. They must show that creative art and higher education are so closely related as to form an integral process. They must find better reasons for the arts in their curriculum than that higher education should reflect popular trends or that because children study art in school they should be able to continue to study it in college. The real test is whether or not the universities can satisfy themselves of a mutually profitable relationship between creative art and liberal learning.

Creative art is the fulfillment of all approaches to art. Though history and criticism are important in themselves and in contexts other than the artistic, their ultimate end ought to be the furtherance of the creative process whether in the individual or in the society of which he is a member. It is easy to identify the pursuit of creative art as a vocational exercise and for universities which offer vocational studies in other subjects to find a comfortable place for it under their roofs. But for those who believe, as I do, that a distinguishing feature of a true university is liberal learning and who see in that kind of learning one of the university's chief sources of strength and reasons for being, the position of creative art in the curriculum becomes more problematical. To organize the study of art in a vocational school in competition with other vocational schools, whether they are connected with universities or not, is one thing. To see it clearly and treat it in vital relationship to liberal learning is quite another. If we can do this, having first recognized the intrinsic supremacy of creative art in its own realm, the union of the fine arts and the universities will be both enduring and fruitful.

Let us first inquire, then, what interest liberal education may have in the fine arts, and carry the inquiry into their creative phase.

Liberal education is supposed to liberate and cultivate a man's innate intellectual and spiritual powers. It is not supposed to make him into a tool but rather to make him the master of tools. It is supposed to awaken and strengthen the humanistic impulses of society at their source, in the individual. This is done by acquainting him with the humanistic achievements of other generations and civilizations as well as of his own, and in making this acquaintance he at once becomes dependent upon art. He uses it in all its forms—poetry, drama, the novel, music, painting, sculpture, and architecture—both as evidence and as interpretation. He employs it as an international language, as a passport through time and space, for its aesthetic discipline and for the insight it gives him into the meaning of life. Yesterday's arts have formed the foundation of today's humanism ever since the humanists of the Renaissance rediscovered the arts of ancient Greece and Rome and thus repaired the broken thread of Western civilization. In this sense art is an old, not a new, element in liberal education.

If the arts had no more than age and tradition behind them their position in the liberal arts curriculum of a modern university would be an honorable one. As it is, their position is a vital one. Notwithstanding the fact that they must prove their case in an age in which the frontiers of science are rapidly expanding and the social sciences are boldly invading fields heretofore within the domain of the arts, the latter have lost nothing of their usefulness. We still turn to them for understanding of the human spirit. In this field no science or social science has yet surpassed the intuitive genius of the artist.

But what of art in its creative phase, the phase that is the subjective expression of the individual artist and defies all objective categories? I would argue that the presence of the creative process alongside the historical and the critical generates a current that gives life to them. We may best appreciate the effect of that current, perhaps, by imagining what the study of science in the universities would be like (or where the sciences would be today) if it were limited to the history of science. The studio is as essential to the study of the arts as the laboratory is to the study of the sciences. Moreover, the discipline imposed by any art grows stronger and more intensive as one strives to master its creative process. This discipline is akin to and in many respects identical with the discipline of the sciences, language, and logic, which have been the core of the liberal arts since their beginning.

Let us take the case of music. In its advanced phases of theory—harmony, counterpoint, form, melody, orchestration—and in its history when studied with reference to these elements, music presents as rigorous a challenge to the human mind and offers it as keen a discipline as any of the subjects conventionally identified with liberal education. Its value can be discounted in comparison with these only out of ignorance of its true nature or out of a false conception of the purpose of liberal education. There is so much music in the air, with so many people listening to it or playing it in some form or other, that both of these mistakes are frequently made, often by individuals who should know better.

Of all fantasies none is greater than the notion of the creative artist in music or any other medium as a capricious Bohemian fashioning his works out of humors and hunches. No art worth hearing or looking at was ever fashioned in any way other than through long and painful submission to one of life's sternest taskmasters. Few apprentices to that taskmaster ever achieved greatness who were not, or did not make themselves in the process, supremely intelligent, cultured, and even learned men. Just as the works of a great artist are useful to liberal education so is the process that produces those works, provided only that it be true to the highest canons of both education and art and not a half-baked form of either or a specious compromise between both. We must look carefully at all purported demonstrations of the compatibility or incompatibility of education and art. Bad art plus good education rule out art. Bad education plus good art rule out education. Bad art plus bad education may find happy union where innocence is bliss or vulgarity reigns. They are fit companions that do not belong in universities. Good art and good education are fit companions that do.

Thus far we have considered the interest of liberal education in creative art. Let us now consider the interest of creative art in liberal education.

We must concede at once that great art is produced only by individuals endowed with great creative gifts and that these are beyond the power of any educational institution to grant or instill. For individuals in whom the gift is prodigious, apprenticeship to a master may be preferable to any form of institutional training. The general self-education of the genius usually comes to embrace most of what he would have got through liberal education in college, and there is no evidence to prove that he would have got this better by the institutional method. Nevertheless, the creative artist is a human being, and what improves him as a human being will improve him as an artist. Through its professional schools, higher education can improve the artist's technical mastery. Equally important is its power to help him interpret experience by illuminating that experience with the light of liberal learning.

Who could gain more from what has been esteemed for two thousand years as the ideal education for the ideal citizen than the artist whose genius enables him to reveal the ideal to his fellow men and inspires him to lead them toward it? C. P. Snow has argued that only by disciplining—and employing—their intellectual powers will novelists be able to prevent their art from declining while science flourishes. For this, he says, "stronger intellects and deeper insights" will be needed. The development and encouragement of intellectual power and the encouragement of its possessors to use it are the business of liberal education. In this, liberal education has as much to offer all artists as it has to offer the members of any profession.

Fundamental, too, in the creative artist's stake in higher education is the enlightenment of his audience. He cannot lead men toward the ideal if they will not follow him, and they will not follow if they cannot understand him. Great art depends upon great patronage of art, whether that be vested in individuals, in groups, or in society generally. It depends upon high standards measured against universals, upon good taste and informed criticism, upon the knowledge and the courage to distinguish good from bad and, moreover, upon the provision of resources to support the good. A society in which these things do not exist is not so likely to produce great art or great artists as a society in which they do: we can document this from our own history. Thus the education of our university undergraduates as future patrons and critics of the arts becomes of the utmost importance to the creative artist, and his stake in such education proportionately increases.

Creative art thus points to higher academic standards for higher education. Great art requires greatness of the listener and the beholder as well as of the artist. To understand Bach or Da Vinci or Shakespeare, to receive the full benefit of their revelations of the ideal, we must rise to their level. We must know at least some of the things they knew, think some of their thoughts, feel some of their feelings, even though we cannot ourselves express them in forms so sublime. Competence of this kind requires hard work, intellectual effort, intelligence, imagination. It does not come to us as we passively look at slides or listen to high-fidelity recordings. Neither does it come from jejune efforts at creativity on the part of individuals to whom the Lord did not vouchsafe the creative gift. Though it may be powerfully

88

stimulated by an artist in residence, it comes fundamentally from intellectual discipline in the context of humanistic learning that is the province of liberal education.

The universities have much to contribute to creative art both through their undergraduate colleges of liberal arts and through their professional schools, especially when the latter draw their water from the same well of liberal learning as the undergraduate colleges. The ancient strife between art and education dies hard, but it is dying. The notion that higher education alienates the artist from his art can be relegated to the legendary realm of Bohemia, whence it originated. We who love statistics may be interested, in this connection, in one which I draw from the experience of my own university. In days gone by, two types of students used to be admitted to its school of music, one fresh out of high school, the other after four years of college. In the course of a study that resulted in making the bachelor of arts degree a standard requirement for all admissions, it was revealed that of the school's graduates who had taken the B.A. before entering the school two thirds were engaged in full-time professional careers in music as compared with only one third of those who had entered directly from high school. It may be that the older age and presumably greater maturity of the college graduates were factors in making their decision in favor of a musical career more firm and lasting. The fact is that higher education did not alienate them from their art.

The artists in residence in the universities fortify my conclusion. They would not have stayed as long as they have, or as contentedly, if they had not discovered fresh fields and pastures new, and they would not have produced the works that have sprung from their genius in the abode of learning if the latter had seduced or distracted them from their art. *Ars non habet inimicum nisi ignorantem* runs the proverb—

"Art has no enemy but an ignorant man." The universities and the fine arts are natural allies.

There is every reason for strengthening their alliance and for expecting, as we do so, that we shall strengthen both its members. And there are particular reasons for doing this now. This is a time of anxiety and doubt which undermine the very foundations of our faith as a free people. Of all forms of education none has fed the roots of that freedom so generously as liberal education, and of all persons to whom freedom is the very breath of life few can compare with the creative artist. Seven years ago Jacques Maritain prophesied in his A. W. Mellon Lectures in the Fine Arts, "Despite the conditions of our present state of civilization, so hostile to creative freedom, there will always be artists who have fortitude enough to turn toward the inner sources and trust in the power of the small translucid cloud of poetic intuition. They will be able to get out of . . . various entanglements . . . and to be unselfish in the very awakening of creative subjectivity." Boris Pasternak has fulfilled this prophecy. So have countless other artists, whose entanglements may not have been as great.

If those artists can show us how to escape from such entanglements, liberal education can show us how to prevent them from being created in the first place. Both artists and educators serve the cause of individual freedom and for this reason if for no other deserve all the support our freedom-hungry society can give them. Without their help, though we may not be enslaved by commissars, we shall be ground to a spiritual pulp in our headlong passion for organization.

Another reason why the universities should stand by and strengthen the fine arts is the very one that compels them to strengthen the sciences. We are living in a time when science is being called upon to save our skins before art can save our souls. I do not in the least minimize our need to strengthen the sciences by every means we can. Yet I am convinced that science alone, unaided by the arts, cannot save us, either as a nation or as a civilization. In both respects our salvation depends not only upon our military prowess but also upon our ability to win the confidence of the free nations and arouse the hopes of the people of the unfree. What those peoples think of us will be as important to our security as our scientific weapons—perhaps more important, as it could obviate the necessity of employing those weapons in a mutually destructive nuclear war.

In making up their minds what they think about us, these people will judge us by our culture, and in the representation of that culture our arts will speak with authority. Already they have proved, even in moments of acute international tension and crisis, that they can unlock doors inaccessible to politics and penetrate where diplomacy cannot enter. They speak the universal language of humanity. It is peculiarly appropriate at this critical juncture in our history that our universities should make their voices heard in that language and contribute in full measure to the great purpose it serves.

"Primitive art," writes Doctor Zhivago, "the art of Egypt, Greece, our own—it is all, I think, one and the same art through thousands of years. You can call it an idea, a statement about life, so all-embracing that it can't be split up into separate words; and if there is so much as a particle of it in any work that includes other things as well, it outweighs all the other ingredients in significance and turns out to be the essence, the heart and soul of the work."

"A statement about life, so all-embracing that it can't be split up into separate words" would make a very good definition of liberal education. We must not deny that education to our artists, and we must certainly not deny to education that which reveals "the essence, the heart and soul of the work."

The Best of Two Worlds: Athletics and Education

The question of the proper relationship between athletics and education is one which no American college or university can ignore and few can answer to their complete satisfaction. Other nations are just as passionately addicted to athletic sports as we are. In most, these sports are organized and pursued, under auspices totally separate and distinct from educational institutions. Even in the British nations, where everybody follows the races and the football pools, and Oxford rows and plays football with Cambridge, universities are nowhere nearly as institutionally involved in athletics as they are in the United States.

How did this situation come about? How did a handful of liberal arts colleges, during the very time they were growing into universities and assuming the intellectual and moral responsibilities of that status become involved in an intercollegiate enterprise that today owns and manages some 100 major football stadiums, many of which would make their classical prototype, the Roman Colosseum, look like a teacup, with a total season's paid attendance of 15 million and aggregate receipts of over $40 million—not to mention basketball arenas with an attendance of 8 million and baseball diamonds, track fields, and rowing facilities in proportion? College football attendance is roughly equal to major league baseball's, and exceeds professional football's by five times. How did all this start? What is it doing to our colleges and universities and what can they do about it?

It started in the love of sport, which anthropology has traced to nearly every people and country in the world, and archaeologists have pushed far back into the pre-Christian era. As modern team sports developed in colleges and universities, physical energies of the undergraduates, which still occasionally spill over in campus riots, were channeled into organized athletics. English and American colleges, with their common attachment to the classics of ancient Greece, found in these specific sanction for physical training as part of the educational process. The very fact that the new sports were organized put a premium on organization to support them; and for this the colleges, with their highly organized and instinctively competitive societies of young men in the prime of athletic age, were made to order. Living together as well as studying together provided a well-nigh perfect environment for the growth of organized athletics as the monasteries once had done for religious meditation.

That organized athletics were in the educational blood stream before the first American colleges were founded is indicated by the fact that Oliver Cromwell, an undergraduate of Sidney Sussex College, Cambridge, in 1616, was afterward reputed to have been "one of the chief matchmakers and players of football, cudgels or any other boisterous sport or game." Football, in those days, was a wild affair, which the Puritan Stubbes described in 1583 as "rather . . . a bloody and murthering practise than a felowly sporte or pastime." His description of the game should give some satisfaction to latter-day athletic reformers:

> For dooth not every one lye in waight for his Adversary, seeking to overthrowe him & to picke him on his nose, though it be uppon hard stones? . . . so that by this meanes, sometimes their necks are broken, sometime their backs, sometime their legs, sometime their armes;

sometime one part thrust out of joynt, sometime an
other; sometime the noses gush out with blood, sometime their eyes start out; and sometimes hurt in one
place, sometimes in another . . . and hereof groweth
envie, malice, rancour, cholor, hatred, displeasure, en-
mitie, and what not els: and sometimes fighting, brawl-
ing, contention, quarrel picking, murther, homicide,
and great effusion of blood, as experience dayly teach-
eth.

Such was the lusty Elizabethan ancestor of the American
game that started with a contest between Harvard and Yale
in 1875. Football even more than baseball or rowing or other
sports was a college original, and remains so notwithstanding
the recent advent of the professional game. The colleges defined its rules, molded it into its modern form, and gave it its
character. More accurately, it was not the colleges that did
these things, it was their undergraduates, acting largely upon
their own initiative as the record shows, with little awareness,
much less control, on the part of their academic officers. In
this fashion by the turn of the century organized athletics
had become a fixture in American higher education.

What shall we say of the results? Organized athletics gave
the colleges a new lease on life, an exciting, enjoyable and
much more healthful alternative to previous forms of student
recreation. They released new energies, infused undergraduate life with new unity and zeal—which, if not prima facie
assets to higher education, certainly strengthened the foundations of the colleges as residential communities. As long as
organized athletics remained within the bounds of amateurism they imparted its object lessons and its values to the
whole community. In these ways they served the general interests of the colleges, educational as well as social. They
have become so much a part of college life that it is hard to

conceive of that life without them, even harder to imagine what might take their place.

Wherein lies the evil? For a time some of it stemmed from playing rules, particularly those of football (which once resembled legalized mayhem); but these have been so much improved as virtually to eliminate this source of trouble. The real evil, the one that has been scotched but not yet killed, lay not in the actual playing of organized athletic sports but in the managing of them.

Managing them was a responsibility that reached out much more widely into other areas than drafting and supervising their playing rules did. Managing them meant, or soon came to mean, catering to spectators as well as to participants. It meant not merely providing players with proper instruction and equipment, scheduling trips, and keeping the books on playing expenses, but calculating grand strategy, staging and producing contests that rapidly assumed the character (and dimensions) of public spectacles, scouting, recruiting and fielding players equal to these public responsibilities—and at the same time ensuring that the academic life of each particular institution continued to prosper. The sheer weight of this problem fell heavily upon a group of institutions inexperienced in such matters and on the whole ill-equipped to deal with them. Most colleges and universities were conscientiously trying to improve their academic standards and many were succeeding in that effort. But as the standards rose, so did the demand for athletic victories and championships, and the two were not always consistent. It was as though the major league baseball teams were suddenly put under levy to win not only the pennants but also Rhodes Scholarships and Nobel Prizes.

To the solution of the problem, moreover, organized athletics brought not cool heads and collected thoughts but the passions of tribal warfare. These were normal enough to the extent that they reflected the competitive spirit of players and their undergraduate supporters. But there was something that gave them an abnormal force. This was the growing interest of spectators and the tendency of the colleges to cater to and commercialize that interest. To the colleges this meant a new source of revenue as well as (they hoped) a new focus of alumni loyalty and public support. To the spectators it meant excitement, thrills, broken records, and victories.

The bargain seemed like a natural one at the time it was struck, mutually profitable and beneficial. Yet it soon imposed on the colleges hidden costs and unforeseen consequences. To keep up revenue and, presumably, alumni loyalty, winning teams were necessary; to be sure of winning teams competent players had to be recruited. If such players required financial inducements, the inducements had to be provided. If academic or amateur standards stood in the way, the standards had to be compromised.

Bit by bit, as the possibilities of revenue-producing sports were exploited, other sports, which meant virtually all save basketball, were budgeted against football. Each budgetary item thus added increased the pressure on coaches, players, athletic directors, presidents, and governing boards to maintain the winning teams that ensured the gate receipts. As the game grew more specialized and the market for players more competitive, the colleges and universities found themselves in a managerial competition as intensive as their rivalry on the field and differing from professional baseball only in its pretensions to amateurism. Competitive methods varied from outright awards of room, board, tuition, and other prerequisites, such as automobiles and spending allowances, to disguised subsidies by alumni; from artificial majors in physical education and even false enrollments in college to individual favors and dispensations by boards of admission, and eligibility and scholarship committees.

This, I think, is the real evil organized athletics inflicted upon our colleges and universities. To label it "overemphasis" barely scratches its surface. Undue deference to spectators has led the colleges to default to a certain extent on their professional competence, to forfeit a measure of their proper authority over their own affairs. This was tantamount to a surrender of academic freedom on the athletic field while this was being defended in the classroom. For some this caused no more than a time-consuming distraction. For others it created a satellite that became a sun.

From the standpoint of education the fact had logical consequences. The main purpose of an educational institution is education. The main purposes of organized athletics are recreation and exercise. Both of these are essential to good work in education as in every other calling. Neither is a substitute for such work, much less its equal or its master. This suggests a line of demarcation, a watershed, on one side of which organized athletics serve the cause of education while on the other they hurt it; and it further suggests that it is the duty of each educational institution to draw that line and defend it. This, after all, is asking no more of educational institutions than the Pure Food and Drug Act requires of the manufacturers of those products or, for that matter, than a major league manager might ask of his players if they kept skipping batting practice to study history.

From the standpoint of athletics as well as education the fact has logical consequences. The aspiration of most American colleges has been to achieve the standing if not the shape and size of universities, and the aspiration of most American universities has been to do full justice to that status. In its original and proper meaning the word university signifies standards—the highest standards of integrity and quality pertaining to their activities anywhere in society. Any trifling with those standards, however slight or for whatever expedient reason, is a contradiction in terms.

97

Since these standards can apply to everything a university does, they apply to athletics as well as to education. The application of the standards to college and university athletics was twofold. In the first place, they were to be amateur athletics, a principle early laid down by the colleges and periodically reaffirmed by their presidents, governing boards, athletic directors, coaches, and team captains, as well as by their various rules committees and intercollegiate associations. The principle was first and last a players' concept. It said nothing about the entertainment of spectators or the raising of college revenue, and it expressly forbade participation for financial or any other material remuneration.

The second standard is succinctly stated in the preamble to the revised Ivy Group Agreement of 1954 for organized athletic programs: "In the total life of the campus, emphasis upon intercollegiate competition must be kept in harmony with the essential educational purposes of the institution."

This was no more than the application to intercollegiate competition of the line of demarcation or watershed that the colleges had adopted for all athletics. It is worth noticing how congenial the first principle, i.e. the amateur, is to the second—so congenial as to suggest that if it were lived up to 100 per cent, the second would be superfluous. For as we have seen, it was precisely in the terms and values of amateurism that organized athletics discovered their most congenial relationship and made their most direct and constructive contributions to "the essential educational purposes of the institution." In more ways than one the amateur principle in athletics was the corollary to liberal education in the classroom.

These principles were not foisted upon our colleges and universities. They grew out of their intrinsic character. Through them the colleges, in addition to devising and refining the techniques of so many of our athletic sports, contributed largely to their moral value to us as a nation. Moreover, the collegiate influence transcended its own sphere to make itself strongly felt through its code of sportsmanship in professional athletics. These, too, have a stake in its survival. When a professional team overcomes a handicap or comes from behind to win against seemingly impossible odds, sportswriters often call it "a Frank Merriwell finish" or "the old college try."

This is more than sentimental—or satiric—metaphor. It it professionalism at its best, earning its highest professional praise in the language and image of amateurism. The colleges have been seduced away from these principles by spectators who as parents and as citizens are their ultimate beneficiaries. Standards that should be pure have been compromised and corrupted, and this is common knowledge among our college students and their faculties. Deliberate departures from principles of this sort cannot fail to damage the reputation of an institution consecrated to truth and excellence by its very charter. Upholding one ideal of truth as applied to education and another as applied to athletics has already caused woeful moral and intellectual confusion in the minds of young men who found themselves subjected to such double standards, not to mention cynicism and disgust in the minds and hearts of their fellow students. This is meager fare from higher education, scarce worth its salt on any pretext. It is hardly consistent with the mottoes of light and truth emblazoned in the arms of our colleges. It is disillusioning and damaging to their good name and to the integrity of their profession.

Are these defects not mitigated by the educational redemption of young men who would not otherwise have come to college? It is possible in individual cases. Yet these can be matched by wholesale departures from college upon the close of their last football season by young men who had absorbed so little of the college's essential purposes and held its educational opportunities in such low esteem that they did not care to complete their courses and graduate; and by other cases, probably more numerous, of bizarre studies that enabled their pursuers to qualify for football or basketball. I have in mind two high school graduates who resigned from an out-of-state university where they held basketball scholarships and played as stars on one of the nation's first ranking basketball teams. One had majored in physical education, the other in recreation. The first told the *New York Times* that he found his academic duties so little demanding that when he was not playing basketball he would go to his room "and just sit there," varying the monotony with movies six times a week, twice on Sundays. This, he said, led him to realize that "there was something more to going to college than playing basketball." The second explained, "I wanted to take a business course but they didn't have one there, so I took the recreation course even though I don't want to be a coach or a teacher. But I realized I couldn't eat the basketball when I finished college."

The holder of an athletic scholarship is in college for one main purpose: to play on the varsity team in the sport for proficiency in which the scholarship was awarded. He enters into a contractural relationship which limits his freedom of choice in athletics as well as in studies. He is restrained from participating in other sports or electing courses which would cut into his time or in any way diminish his usefulness to the varsity, and he is commonly obliged to forfeit the scholarship in case he cannot fulfill his obligations because of injury, or for any other reason. All of this makes slim collateral for claims of educational redemption.

But could the colleges and universities afford to take the loss, the diminution of gate receipts that it is assumed would follow their universal adoption and enforcement of the amateur principle? I am not so sure that they would have to. In the first place, I am not so sure that their student bodies could not produce teams of sufficient caliber, and that within their various leagues and conferences those teams could not engage in sufficiently keen and exciting competition to retain the interest of most of their present spectators. Teams of roughly equal size and strength playing according to the same amateur rules have repeatedly demonstrated their ability to thrill spectators, making up in drama all that they lack in technical finesse.

Suppose worse came to worst and a major refinancing of college athletics became necessary. I doubt that the cost would exceed or even equal the price the colleges are now paying in the corruption of amateur and educational standards and the harm this is doing to both. Why, in any case, should football be taxed with the support of nearly all the other sports? Charging everything to football puts an egregiously unfair pressure upon that game to do just as it has done, to go professional in disguise: and whose fault was this, football's or the colleges'?

The whole concept of farming athletics out to pay for themselves is difficult to reconcile with the meaning and principles of a university. According to these, as we have seen, a single set of standards applied not only to education but to everything a university did, including athletics. The administrative corollary is that athletics and education belong on the same budget and under the same administrative direction; and the stronger the educational claims put forward by athletics, the greater the force of this corollary. The total annual expenditures of all American institutions of higher education is somewhere in the neighborhood of $2.5 billion. Their total gross receipts from football, with a paid attendance of 15 million at an average charge of from $2.50 to $3.00 per ticket would be between $37 million and $45 million. Taking the larger figure for the sake of argument, it represents just about 2 per cent of the income available for these expenditures . . . not, I should think, a sum so great that it could not be rebudgeted and administered in accordance with these principles.

What prospects are there that the step will be taken? The answer is beyond my province. I merely wish to record my belief that it can be done. For this belief I have two basic reasons. The first is that there is nothing inherent in organized athletics themselves to prevent it. I have said they brought the colleges some evil and I have identified the worst of that evil as the separation of academic authority from academic responsibility under spectator pressure. But it was the spectators who drove the wedge, not the athletics. And the spectators are we ourselves, as a nation, as college alumni, and as sports lovers. What we have done we can undo.

The second reason for my faith is that I happen to belong to a group of colleges among which these things are happening. These are not unrepresentative institutions. Most of them have run the whole gamut of experience recorded in these pages. All, including my own, have plenty of unfinished business on their hands that must take precedence over any claims to perfection. Yet all have set their course in this direction, as charted in the Ivy Group Agreement. I can think of no better fate for amateur athletics and higher education than that the members of the Ivy Group live up to those provisions and prove by so doing their universal practicability. To assist them in this they may count on strong allies from education. They will draw inner strength from thriving intramural programs, and their task will be lightened by the continued progress of professional athletics. But their strongest ally now as always will be the courage of their own convictions.

The Alumnus as Patron
of Learning

What are the responsibilities of a university alumnus? To answer the question it will be necessary, in this age of imagery, to dispose of certain images. In fact, it will be necessary to get rid of imagery altogether, to recognize that being an alumnus is not playing a histrionic role arbitrarily assigned by some mysterious casting director; that it is not an act but a fact, an objective reality of great potential consequence to our universities and our country. We must take a hammer to the two most popular images of the American alumnus in the eyes of his countrymen, the clown capering before the façade of learning the interior of which is never revealed either to himself or to his audience; and the irascible member of the old guard who neither dies nor surrenders, fuming with rage (and perhaps a little bourbon) at his football tickets, or the coach, and dashing off sulphurous letters to his university beginning, "I was shocked to discover that" and ending "Unless something is done about this at once I shall no longer contribute or remain, Sincerely yours."
It is true that for a long time the graduates of our colleges and universities have felt it incumbent upon themselves to communicate with one another, as alumni, in the manner and discourse of juveniles at play. Who started this custom or how much it may have retarded American higher education I know not. I only know that whatever validity the image of the alumnus inspired by the custom may have held it is now outdated: where time has not run out on it it is running fast. As to the critic with the low boiling point who does

not hesitate to consign the whole university to damnation because one particular part or aspect of it displeases him, he manages to keep up with the times; but his image is no more faithful to the whole truth than that of the clown.

Even in the past, these images were misleading. For with all the clowning and related excesses of alumni interest in universities for their entertainment value, bearing fruit in the corruption of both athletics and education, and for all the attacks of the self-appointed critics who wrote their universities off as total losses or in righteous indignation consigned them to limbo, it was the alumni of these institutions who from the beginning built them up to what they are today. From the ranks of these alumni serving their own and each other's institutions have come not only the financial benefactors and supporters but also the founders, presiding officers, governing boards, and faculties of the very colleges and universities that were mocked and corrupted by the clown and his followers and damned by the disaffected.

These facts are too often overlooked. The role of the alumnus is not limited to heckling or passing the hat. It carries over into the most sensitive and vital phases of the operation of our system of higher education. He has other responsibilities, to be sure, responsibilities rising in degree with the degree of his own education and extending over the whole range of citizenship in a free society, including its aesthetic and spiritual as well as its political needs. To all such responsibilities the times lend a special urgency, reënforcing the philosophy propounded by the founders of our country upon which our educational system rests. But transcending all is the responsibility of the alumnus for the source which nourishes and sustains that system, namely higher education.

How then shall he discharge that responsibility? There are as many particular ways as there are particular needs and opportunities in higher education. There is one general way, namely, to keep on educating himself. That, after all, is the main purpose of the education he has had to date. It is the special purpose of liberal education. This purpose is not fulfilled by the passing of tests and awarding of degrees. In a sense it is never fulfilled. For it calls upon all who have partaken of it to continue, of their own free will, to extend their knowledge and improve their understanding and use of that knowledge for their own benefit and the benefit of humanity. Its ultimate concern is not mastery of today's knowledge. It is one's capacity—and desire—to think and learn for himself, that will give him mastery of tomorrow's knowledge and make him a contributor to it. To the extent that the education the alumnus has received from his university has enlarged that capacity and cultivated that desire in him, it has been a success. If it has not done either, it has been a failure. The final proof rests with him.

The notion of finality in education mistakes both the meaning of the word and the meaning of the process. The word means a continuous drawing out which is precisely the nature of the process. Parents, teachers, and students are the original partners in it, but as it progresses, more and more of the initiative passes to the student until he is finally on his own.

It is against this time that his university education is intended to prepare the alumnus. When the time comes, however, he will not be able to draw upon the contents of that education as he would upon a savings account. The questions he will have to answer will not be the ones to which he has, or thinks he has, the answers when he graduates. Their substance will change, in politics no less surely than in science. The old labels will not fit, the old textbooks will be as much out of date as those his father studied are today. Party platforms will be forgotten. Even those two inveterate and ageless antagonists, the Conservative and the Liberal, or as Emerson identified them in his famous essay, the party of Conservatism and that of Innovation, will have found something to quarrel over quite different in substance from what they are quarreling over today, just as what they now quarrel over differs from what they quarreled over in Emerson's time, or in 1896 or 1912 or 1932, to cite three particularly quarrelsome years in the more recent past. In our time, which is one of scientific and technological revolution touching off world-wide political, economic, and social revolution, the rate of change is exceptionally fast, its effects exceptionally dramatic. The competence and usefulness with which he pursues his calling and leads his life in these circumstances will depend upon his continuous, purposeful, and industrious self-education; this in turn will be both proof of the value of higher education to him and warranty for his trusteeship of it.

This is by no means a joyless prospect. It does not summon the alumnus to a frantic scramble up intellectual cliffs in which the communists take the hindmost. In addition to life and liberty it has to do with the pursuit of happiness. Although the philosophers have fallen out with one another through the ages over everything else, they have testified with great unanimity to the delights of learning. If he is not yet ready to accept this testimony at face value, I predict that when he graduates, his own efforts at self-education will convince him, that experience will lead him to those delights.

By now the larger dimensions of my subject should have begun to appear. The primary responsibility of an alumnus is the welfare of higher education. The United States and its friends in the free world are looking to higher education for their salvation. The older nations are counting on it to preserve their freedom, the younger ones to establish their freedom. In this community, American higher education bears the heaviest burden. Thus by preparing himself, through self-education, to further the interests of American higher education, the alumnus is preparing himself to render service of first importance, both to his country and to the world.

Further Obsequies
for the Grammarian

Just over a hundred years ago, Robert Browning, in *A Grammarian's Funeral*, paid tribute to the revival of learning that brought an end to the dark ages and ushered western civilization into its present epoch. The hero of the poem is a scholar whose dedication to his scholarly pursuits transcends all earthly gratifications, comforts, friendships, even crippling physical afflictions, and brings him at the end to a kind of Nirvana. In a stumbling cadence that matches their footsteps, the poet speaks his funeral oration through the lips of disciples carrying the corpse of their master up a mountainside for burial. "Our low life was the level's and the night's," the disciples say as they struggle upwards, "he's for the morning . . ."

> Yea, this in him was the peculiar grace
>   (Hearten our chorus!)
> That before living he'd learn how to live—
>   No end to learning:
> Earn the means first—God surely will contrive
>   Use for our earning.
> Others mistrust and say, "But time escapes:
>   Live now or never!"
> He said, "What's time? Leave Now for dogs and apes!
>   Man has Forever. . . .

These lines were published in 1855. How many of us would subscribe to them today? Do we have Forever? Not even dogs and apes can hope to survive the dreadful terminus we fear. Had we not better share Now with them as fully as we can, gnaw on their bones, nibble their fruit? Why not dismiss the whole poem as a period piece, more rhyme than reason and not always that much rhyme, the accidental harmony of nineteenth-century moral earnestness and thirteenth-century asceticism, of little significance to our time.

No harmony is accidental, and there are no dead languages or ancient worlds among poets and philosophers. Though harmony may be discovered by chance, it cannot be thus created. The wandering fingers on the keyboard stumble upon a consonance. The tyro thinks he has invented it, as Chanticleer thought he caused the sun to rise. The musician knows he has merely proved a physical law. The consonance will be there through the ages, in all the nations of the earth, waiting for those who know where to look for it and who understand its meaning. It is a timeless and a universal truth. Such is the language of poets and philosophers. It is never dated, never isolated.

The validity of this poem is as great for our time as it was for its hero's or its author's—if anything, greater: it is enhanced by the very urgency that seems to contradict it. The accolade the poet bestows upon the scholar, the lofty praise for his intellectual striving, his spiritual dedication, and his moral courage, is punctuated by maxims as earthy and as timely as if they had been written this morning.

> Oh, if we draw a circle premature,
> Heedless of far gain,
> Greedy for quick returns of profit, sure
> Bad is our bargain!

The force of this admonition penetrates the thickest mental hedges we have planted to screen unpleasant realities out of our contemporary landscape. The grammarian personi- fies the spirit of true learning in any age. Without that spirit, without liberating and putting to work that measure of it which God has vouchsafed to our portion of the hu- man race, we shall not have Forever and we may not even have Now.

I do not mean to summon the grammarian as one more witness in favor of improving the teaching of science in high school or increasing federal appropriations for space travel and rocket research. Instead, I propose a pilgrimage to the mountain peak where his disciples have left him "still loftier than the world suspects," in order that we may revere him and in that act of reverence find our own sal- vation.

There is no lack of opportunity for learning among us. What is lacking is a respect for it—not the unctuous respect that trails its possessors with diplomas and titles, but an honest respect such as we now have for technical compe- tence or business success. We honor learning but do not believe in it. We reward it with lengthy obituaries and a wretched living wage. Rather than submit to it ourselves we hire substitutes; rather than cultivate our own brains we pick theirs. We spend as much time and energy on short cuts to learning and imitations of learning as we do on learning itself. I once was shown a portion of a silk shirt that a Chinese student some hundred or more years ago had fashioned into a "crib sheet" for use in a civil service examination. I can think of few more laborious processes than tracing microscopic Chinese characters on a piece of silk with a single hair of a brush. If the student had put that much effort into his subject the chances are he would not have needed the crib, and he certainly would have known more about the subject in the end. The case sums up our approach to learning in a shirt tail.

Now we are frightened, unsure of the soundness of these ways, uncertain how to correct them. The curtain has fallen upon our "long apprenticeship to the learning of other lands" not, as Emerson hoped, lowered by our own hands to be raised deliberately on a sturdier native growth, but rung down abruptly by the Russians; not because American culture had fulfilled its promise to ourselves and to the world, but because learning, so slow to find a place of honor in that culture, was suddenly discovered as a strategic asset. Once it had been established in that category we could no longer count on imports to supply it: the risk of being trapped in a showdown by enemies armed with tomorrow's technology was too great. We would have to develop the source of that technology at home.

Thrown upon our own resources, what did we find? We found that we could no longer rely, as we had so often relied in the past, on our frontier spirit to see us through this predicament, for we are no longer a frontier society. The frontier has moved away to other parts of the world, to the poles, to the moon, into outer space. The mere process of living in America has not imbued us with the hardy virtues with which it imbued our pioneer ancestors. On the contrary, conditions of life are easier here than in most of the countries that sent us those pioneers. Moreover, even in its heyday, the frontier did not produce the kind of competence we need now. Thus, by the process of elimination, we rediscovered our much patronized yet more neglected educational system. Thus the affairs of our schools and universities were brought out into the open and submitted to the same agonizing reappraisal as our economy after the crash of 1929 and our military strategy after Pearl Harbor.

This does not mean that we have been converted to

learning as the grammarian exemplified it. We may conclude that a step has been taken in that direction, and call it an ill wind that blows nobody any good. But if we are to realize the full benefit learning might confer upon our civilization the process of conversion has just begun. In the first place, the problem of our survival as a civilization is very much more than a military problem and learning has very much more to contribute to its solution than data of purely military significance. Although it is customary nowadays to construe every human act and thought as an exercise in a manual of arms, there are still some items on our agenda, and among them strategic items of the first magnitude, that require other than military treatment. The security of the United States depends as much upon the degree to which our culture and our way of life command the respect of the free nations and hold out hope to the people of the unfree as it does upon our ability to overawe and impress either by military prowess or races in interstellar space. The rueful reports of American diplomats abroad contrasting with the receptions accorded American artists in countries whence these reports emanate suggest that we have much to learn in this respect. The American image of Now is a more important factor in the cold war than we think it is. It is said that when the cannon are silent the muses are heard. May not the reverse also be true, that when the muses are heard the cannon are silent? And might these not be our muses (and cannon) and other peoples' cannon (and muses)?

But I am putting the grammarian on the witness' stand in spite of myself. We need learning not only to protect our national security but also for the reason that he craved it—in order that we may know how to live our own lives. As science extends our conquest of the physical world and pushes its frontiers farther and farther beyond the realm of common human knowledge and experience, we must call on the wisdom of humanistic learning if we are truly to profit by those gains. Both types of learning are essential to us as a nation and as individual members of our race, and each is essential to the other.

Recognizing their mutual importance, I take the liberty of reminding you that Browning's hero was after all a grammarian, not a scientist. I do this not out of academic partisanship but in order that I may lay further stress upon the mutual dependence of humanistic and scientific learning. In modern professional idiom the grammarian would be identified as a linguist, perhaps a philologist, a master of all the intricacies of form and usage of language. As such he would be the enemy of jargon, the nemesis of the demagogue and the hidden persuader. I feel sure, for example, that he would have been able to distinguish between an oversized, overpowered motor vehicle and a prestige symbol, and that he would be able to communicate this skill to his disciples. I feel equally sure that he would know the full derivation and meaning of the words "freedom" and "responsibility" and that he would understand clearly the difference between the study of the English language and literature and the study of journalism, radio speaking and broadcasting, or any of the scores of substitutes now available, and would entertain no illusions about the respective effects of such studies upon the American mind.

Important as all these gains would be to a society in which learning is less esteemed than loquacity, I have yet to demonstrate the mutual dependence of the grammarian and the scientist. I might do this by referring to the liberal arts which for two thousand years have embraced them both in a common curriculum. But in so doing I might lay myself open to attack as a traditionalist. I shall therefore resort to parable. One of the skills of which the grammarian would be master is rhetoric. Whether we define this, after the scholars of more recent times, as the principles and rules of composition, or with Plato, as the art of persuasion, it is a potent weapon in the hands of its possessor. Down through the ages it has served various masters. It has disciplined the mind of the scholar in exactitude and truth, and it has armed the demagogue in his conquest of the innocent. At times it has subjected both to its control, as we have seen it do in the form of Marxian dialectic.

In the grammarian's possession, rhetoric would be devoted to exactitude and truth. How important this would be to the modern scientist and his world may be illustrated from the experience of Socrates' disciple Gorgias:

> A marvel, indeed, Socrates, if you only knew how rhetoric comprehends and holds under her sway all the inferior arts. Let me offer you a striking example of this. On several occasions I have been with my brother Herodicus or some other physician to see one of his patients, who would not allow the physician to give him medicine, or apply a knife or hot iron to him; and I have persuaded him to do for me what he would not do for the physician just by the use of rhetoric.

The dialogue continues:

> SOCRATES: You were saying, in fact, that the rhetorician will have greater powers of persuasion than the physician even in a matter of health?
> GORGIAS: Yes, with the multitude,—that is.
> SOCRATES: You mean to say, with the ignorant; for with those who know he cannot be supposed to have greater powers of persuasion.
> GORGIAS: Very true.

SOCRATES: But if he is to have more power of persuasion than the physician, he will have greater power than he who knows?

GORGIAS: Certainly.

SOCRATES: Although he is not a physician:—is he?

GORGIAS: No.

SOCRATES: And he who is not a physician must, obviously, be ignorant of what the physician knows.

GORGIAS: Clearly.

SOCRATES: Then, when the rhetorician is more persuasive than the physician, the ignorant is more persuasive with the ignorant than he who has knowlledge?—is not that the inference?

The rhetorician is always more persuasive than the physician and today has at his command such cunning arts of communication that he may take the world for his patient. Will he take ours, prescribing the knife here, the hot iron there, in his capricious quackery? His instrument is more potent than the hydrogen bomb, his orbit greater than the satellites. In determining our future he is at least the partner of the scientist, and at most his master. What guarantee do we have that he will use his powers wisely? "I would rather begin by asking," says Socrates, "whether he is or is not as ignorant of the just and unjust, base and honourable, good and evil, as he is of medicine and the other arts." And in another place he instructs one of his disciples to go and tell the rhetoricians "that if their compositions are based on knowledge of the truth, and they can defend or prove them, when they are put to the test, by spoken arguments, which leave their writings poor in comparison of them, then they are to be called, not only poets, orators, legislators, but are worthy of a higher name, befitting the serious pursuit of their life . . . lovers of wisdom or philosophers is their modest and befitting title."

Of such clay was our grammarian. To him rhetoric could be entrusted in the sure knowledge that he would use it as a defense against quackery rather than a device for practicing it, that he would employ it as a tool for the clearer understanding and better enjoyment of Now in the perspective of Forever. I salute him and the poet who has preserved the inspiration of his example for a nation sorely in need of it.

The Creative Individual

With our search for a balance between moral responsibility and scientific progress, we renew man's immemorial effort to find his place as an individual in a world that seems to recognize him only as a species. Since that moment, lost in the mists of time, when man first looked upon himself and saw the image of God, he has struggled against all the powers of nature and the supernatural, and against all the tyrannies of his fellow men, to fulfill the promise in that image. He has lived to the full, in pleasure and pain, the gregarious life to which half of his instincts and appetites committed him. And, in response to the other half, he has striven in every element on earth, in the skies above the earth, and in the waters under the earth, to express himself as an individual.

Philosophers have long recognized this centrifugal conflict in the bosom of man, and we, like every generation before us, have been witnesses to its political manifestations. Our world is divided between political philosophies proclaiming man's mechanistic fate as a species and those which proclaim his creative destiny as an individual. At the moment the mechanistic idea seems to be in the ascendant. It is propagated at the point of the sword by dictatorships now governing nearly half the peoples of the world and seeking to extend their dominion over the rest. It is given credence among the free peoples either because of their poverty, which depresses them, or because of their secret weapons and their automatic machines, which mystify and baffle them. Never in history, or so it seems to us, has the individual defended his birthright against such formidable odds.

Yet he has not resigned from the human race. On the contrary, neither science nor technology nor all the deterministic doctrine inspired by them, nor the despotisms that have tried to force that doctrine upon mankind, have succeeded in producing a world that can function without our individual powers of reason, imagination, and conscience. We are not mere sponges or plankton afloat on a tide of causation over which we have no control. We are rational beings, capable of charting the tide, and navigating it, and even diverting and directing it. There is no dialectical or technological substitute for the creative individual.

Whence come our doubts and hallucinations in this regard? They come partly from fear, partly from laziness. We are afraid that where, as in Soviet Russia, there is mystery there is also magic; that the Russians have possessed themselves of some supernatural means of enslaving the will of men; that they will blow us all to bits by methods unknown to western science. We have beguiled ourselves with gadgets, with machines that work for us, and think for us, and entertain us, and (as we believe in our folly) educate us, until our God-given individual powers have become atrophied through disuse. In this hypnotic state we have fallen prey to some of the very teachings we profess to abhor, the teachings of those who proclaim the world machine blueprinted in the Kremlin and the atomizing of the human race without the assistance of the bomb.

The last World War and the terrible weapons now in existence give us abundant reason to fear the next; and the ruthless and aggressive tactics of the Kremlin around the world give us every reason to think that the Russians are willing to gamble on it. But there is no reason in the unreasoning dread that exalts them into supermen and credits their doctrines with wonder-working properties. And as for the television sets that take us from our books, the business machines that clatter away under wall mottos reading "THINK," the electrical examination correctors that dispense with writing, the inner-spring mattresses that end up in bed boards, and the prefabricated knowledge that ends in remedial reading—for all this childish fascination with gadgetry we have only childishness as an excuse. Nor do science and the industrial revolution now projecting itself into the atomic age, afford any better excuse. For whereas the first social interpreters of these phenomena were responsible for the idea of the submergence of the individual, modern scientists are the leaders in repudiating it.

What is it that makes each generation so sure that its own set of circumstances is unique and yet forms a basis for universal preachments and predictions? The Bible says it is the essential vanity of man. I should say it is his innocence of history, of the cumulative experience of his fellow men. We are forever calculating our prospects on the strength of a mere peep through a knothole at this experience. So early economists who observed the first sensational progress of the industrial revolution deduced their concept of economic man, which the scientific socialists appropriated and developed into the full-blown doctrine of economic determination. The whole dialectical process is barely a hundred years old, and the leading figure in it was Karl Marx.

Let us concede that Marx chose an exceptional knothole—the British Museum—that he brought to it an exceptional intellectual apparatus, and that he kept his eye

to it (day after day for nearly thirty-five years) with exceptional perseverance. His range of vision was still exceptionally limited. Man made his debut on the planet in the Pleis-
tocene epoch of the Cenozoic era, about a million years
ago. From the time he took up farming, in the Neolithic
age, about 7,000 B.C., his experiences have been relevant
to modern economic society. There is every reason to extend this perspective TO A.D. 7,000, if not to A.D. 1,000,000.
Marx's focal depth included little more than a bookish
version of the industrial revolution in England between the
years 1820 and 1860, with the preponderance of his evidence drawn from the earlier rather than the later part
of that period. That is to say, Marx took as the verification
of his hypothesis a static view of conditions in one country,
already undergoing change while he wrote, and offered it
to the world as both timeless and universal. Nor was his
view entirely objective. Marx was a bitter, vindictive, un-
happy man, suffering the plagues of Job without Job's
faith, tortured by poverty and disease, living in squalor,
so proud and thin-skinned, as one of his biographers tells
us, that he made excessive demands on the world and when
these were not satisfied (as they nearly always were not)
turned in upon himself "in paroxysms of hatred and of
rage." Yet it is this static, myopic, misanthropic view of human experience that is offered as the principal foundation
for the belief that the machine is all and the individual
is nothing, and for the Communist dictatorship that exploits that belief to suit its purposes. It has all the eerie
aspects of those prehistoric Siberian mammoths frozen into
the ice with hair and flesh intact, with everything, that is,
except life and sense.

One would think that the very nature of Marx's vision
would make it suspect; that the influence of his own baleful
personality contradicted his own thesis; that the direct, per-

sonal influence of Lenin on the outcome of the Russian revolution (suppose the German High Command had never let him cross Germany in a sealed-up boxcar) contradicted it even more emphatically; and that the fact that the thesis has to be maintained by tyranny and enforced by secret police contradicted it finally and flatly. Dialectical materialism has been refuted by the very unfolding of history that Marx and Engels claimed would support it. The industrial revolution has not steadily diminished but steadily increased labor's share of the wealth it produces until, in the industrial countries of western Europe and North America, this share has risen to 80 per cent of the net national product—exactly the opposite of what Marx and his followers predicted. Their theory, says the British economist Colin Clark, "is so flatly contradicted by all the facts that those who propagate it must be very ignorant men, or unfortunately, in a few cases, well-informed men who are deliberately setting out to pervert the truth." Communism has struck its deepest roots not among highly industrialized nations, as Marx confidently predicted it would, but among underdeveloped agrarian nations. It has resulted not in the withering away of the state but in the most highly regimented despotism in history. If Marxism had to survive on its merits, it would perish. It survives only as an orthodoxy imposed by force.

There remains our awe of science and the technology of our own time. Here we observe the mechanical performance of human skills on a constantly ascending plane of rationality that could end either in consummation of man's long struggle for freedom or in a mere exchange of inhuman for human masters. Scientific knowledge has no theoretical limit. A century ago disease and famine were accepted as inevitable and explained away as fate or as the postulates of deterministic philosophy. On the frontiers of scientific knowledge today nothing is inevitable save birth and death. Science, once accused of robbing man of his free will, seems to be giving it back to him.

Our scientists speak of steadily broadening horizons for the creative individual and of the urgent need for him to press on toward those horizons. "Man has risen, not fallen," writes George Gaylord Simpson in *The Meaning of Evolution*. "He can choose to develop his capacities as the highest animal and try to rise still further, or he can choose otherwise. The choice is his responsibility, and his alone. There is no automism that will carry him upward without choice or effort and there is no trend solely in the right direction. Evolution has no purpose; man must supply this for himself." To do so, to make the wise choice for himself and his fellow men, is the ethical responsibility of man which he must discharge as an individual if he is ever going to realize its benefits as a species.

But, we say, can we not entrust this responsibility to others, to the elaborate teams of specialists that are constantly producing new techniques, new tools, and—may we not assume—new visions of wisdom and justice? What do the scientists say to this? I suppose there is no more impressive example of team work in human history than that which produced the atomic bomb. Listen to the opinion of one of the world's outstanding scholars in that field, Percy Bridgman, whose researches in nuclear physics won him the Nobel Prize in 1946. So elaborate has the organization, equipment, and administrative detail become, writes Professor Bridgman, that each team of physicists "has to be driven by some one at the head who has the ideas. There is danger here that all the rest of the team will pick the brains of one man, with an ultimate decrease in the number of physicists in the community capable of independent and critical thought." And he goes on to say:

121

The participation of the individual is necessary in every process of intelligence, not merely in the processes of science. Intelligence can be given a meaning only in terms of the individual. It seems to me that this has a far-reaching significance not usually appreciated, for I believe that here is to be found perhaps the most compelling justification for democracy. Intelligence is based on the individual. An authoritarian society in which the individual is suppressed cannot, by the nature of intelligence, be characterized by *general* intelligence.

The mood that exalts the machine is an aberration. Time and again we have seen the individual apparently ready to exit from the stage only to have him change his mind, or to return, with fresh and more dynamic lines and a whole new development of the plot. We had communism in the Plymouth Colony in 1620, two centuries before Marx wrote his *Manifesto* and three centuries before the Russians ever heard of it, and gave it up, after a pragmatic test, because, as Governor Bradford wrote in his diary,

> The experience that was had in this commone course and condition, tried sundry years, and that amongst godly and sober men, may well evince the vanities of that conceite of Platos and other ancients, applauded by some of later times;—that the taking away of propertie, and bringing in communitie into a comone wealth, would make them happy and florishing; as if they were wiser then God. For this comunitie (so farr as it was) was found to breed much confusion and discontent, and retard much imployment that would have been to their benefite and comforte.

We had totalitarianism, complete with purges and secret police, in the Massachusetts Bay Colony, three centuries before Hitler, Stalin, and Mussolini; we gave it up in revulsion, and drafted statutes and constitutions to prevent its recurrence in the future.

In our traffic with foreign nations we have always looked out on a world full of despotisms. When was it ever not so? As colonies we were their pawns. As a young republic we were surrounded by them, and if the airplane had been invented a century earlier than it actually was invented, the chances are we would still be their pawn. Democracy is a very new thing in the world. Our knowledge of man in society goes back to the Neolithic age nine thousand years ago. Over that span of time man has seen and suffered despotisms of every conceivable variety. We read their epitaph in Shelley's "Ozymandias."

Democracy, the hopeful philosophy, attuned to man's instincts as an individual and addressed to their cultivation for the benefit of society, first appeared in Athens about 500 B.C., saw fitful revival in the Italian city states of the eleventh and twelfth centuries A.D., and later in the Swiss cantons, but did not make its modern appearance until the Puritan revolution in England in the middle years of the seventeenth century. It did not attain the form in which we know it until the nineteenth century. Compared with despotism it is but a few minutes old. The remarkable fact is not that it is still opposed by despotism but that it has survived that opposition as vigorously as it has.

It has survived because time and again it has proved, under stress, its ability to harmonize and make productive in every sphere of thought and action the individual and the social instincts innate in man. In these respects it had demonstrated its superiority over all other political philosophies. All try to draw the line between the opportunities and responsibilities of the individual and those of society, but none draws it so subtly in accordance with reality as democracy. And what is that reality? It is that for nine thousand years society has depended upon its members as individuals for those creative achievements of mind and spirit that have guided it along the path of civilization. The spark from heaven falls. Who picks it up? The crowd? Never. The individual? Always. It is he and he alone, as artist, inventor, explorer, scholar, scientist, spiritual leader, or statesman, who stands nearest to the source of life and transmits its essence to his fellow men. Let them tie his hands or stop his mouth or dragoon him in the name of uniformity, and they cut themselves off from that source in equal measure.

Wisdom and virtue cannot be forced from a crowd as eggs are from chickens under electric lights. There is no such thing as general intelligence. There is only individual intelligence communicating itself to other individual intelligences. And there is no such thing as public morality, there is only a composite of private morality. The Athenian statesman Pericles perceived these truths when he said of democracy in its earliest phase that it trusted "less in system and policy than to the native spirit of our citizens." And so did Thomas Jefferson, on the threshold of our own age, when he wrote, "It is the manners and spirit of a people which preserve a republic in vigor." The same could be said of all forms of government, but of none so truly as that in which the voice of the people is the voice of God.

This is another way of saying, is it not, that democracy is fundamentally a moral philosophy, a fact which, more than any other in its nature and history, has enabled it to survive all of its previous incarnations. This is as true now in the atomic age as it was in the age of Pericles. It is a truth whose consequences will be read when archaeologists dig up the remains of our civilization. If they there find images like Shelley's Ozymandias it will be because we have failed to cultivate our powers at the source. We have the means for this in the most far-reaching system of education any free people has ever known, a system created and developed expressly for this purpose. We have the material resources to enable this system to fulfill its purpose without diverting a penny from the essential needs of our armed forces or from any other national interest of comparable importance. The problem is to create the will.

In the solution of this problem hangs the fate of our nation and our civilization. For the very scientific progress that some think spells the doom of democracy depends for its vitality on two things: first, the continuing discoveries of individuals in the realm of pure science, hence the continuing educational process that produces those individuals; and second, a social philosophy that converts the human energy newly rescued from drudgery by technological advances to uses consistent with this purpose. This vast store of energy, exceeding in human terms our greatest accomplishment in the conservation of natural resources, in military and political terms equivalent to the enlistment of a powerful new ally in the defense of democracy, is at hand and ready to use. How shall we use it? Shall we abandon it to the entertainment industry? Shall we neglect it while we accuse one another of treason, like the farmer in the Bible who spent so much time pulling up tares he harvested no ripe wheat? Shall we forget it in our fear of the ideas of a group of Russian doctrinaires, isolated even from their own people? If we do these things we shall have to answer for them just as surely as the broken statue of Ozymandias in the Egyptian desert answers for all bodies politic that hold their individual members in contempt.

The Limited Competence
of the State

The growth of the state throughout the world has been a commonplace of our times. First in Russia, then in Italy and Germany, then receding from western Europe but spreading into China, the tide of totalitarian dictatorship seems to have been continuously at the flood. For nearly seventeen years our country has been in a condition of full or partial mobilization, for seven years actually at war, to keep this flood from our shores. Meanwhile the free nations have themselves experienced remarkable accretions in the power of the state. Not only those nations whose history and traditions were less democratic, but also Great Britain and the United States, the two nations whose intimately related political and social institutions form the very vertebrae of modern democracy, have all seen public enterprise move into many areas heretofore occupied by private. To perceive the change in our own case one has but to compare the federal payroll of 1953 with that of 1933, or, for that matter, both major party platforms of 1952 with those of 1932.

A world of difference separates the two kinds of state expansion. While I do not intend to dwell on this difference, neither do I wish to minimize it. I do not see how anyone who understands the Constitution of the United States and the history that brought it forth and subsequently refined it can fail to look upon any form of totalitarian dictatorship as utterly abhorrent. Nor can I see how anyone with so much as an armchair knowledge of history can fail to comprehend the extent of the difference between the system of government prevailing among Soviet Russia and her satellites and the systems prevailing among the free nations, particularly in the United States. By the same token I am concerned with the way in which the authority of the state has expanded at home, and I hope that when this question is presented to you as citizens you will once and for all live down your reputation as a silent generation.

Democracy is the most versatile and resourceful of governments. It has proved itself capable of rising to any occasion, assuming any shape from a laissez-faire economy in time of peace and plenty to a highly efficient military machine in wartime. But there is one principle it can never compromise nor long suspend. This is the principle of the separation of powers. The roots of this principle lie deep in the history of democracy. Madison, in *The Federalist,* called it the "essential precaution in favor of liberty" and "the sacred maxim of free government." "The accumulation of all powers, legislative, executive, and judiciary, in the same hands, whether of one, a few, or many, and whether hereditary, self-appointed, or elective, may justly be pronounced the very definition of tyranny." "It is by balancing each of these powers against the other two," wrote John Adams, "that the efforts in human nature towards tyranny can alone be checked and restrained, and any degree of freedom preserved in the Constitution." Jefferson attached equal weight to the principle. Thus spoke a generation that feared above all the tyranny of the legislature, that expected the tyranny of the executive to come in its day, that set itself against tyranny of all kinds and can

127

now claim a hundred and fifty years of our hindsight to the credit of its foresight. Is this not good reason for asking ourselves whether, in extending the powers and functions of government in the United States, we have faithfully observed—and are now observing—this principle?

But there is a still larger sense in which the growth of the state in a democracy should be a matter of concern to its citizens. There is a yet greater separation of powers that must be observed. What, after all, is the object of political society? Its end and purpose, says Aristotle, "is the good life, and the institutions of social life are means to that end." He defines that good life as "a life of true felicity and goodness"; and he goes on to say, "It is therefore for the sake of good actions, and not for the sake of social life, that political associations must be considered to exist."

This was certainly true of the political association formed in Philadelphia in the summer of 1787. Its founders recognized clearly that government was but one, nor at that the noblest, of several means to their end. ("But what is government itself," says *The Federalist,* "but the greatest of all reflections on human nature? If men were angels no government would be necessary.") They understood both the necessity and the limitations of law. On the near, the safe, side of the fences they erected against tyranny they expected more than mere security for the individual, much more than mere freedom. They expected him to develop his innate qualities of morality and intelligence and to convert these into actions. To these ends they looked upon religion and education as means distinct and separate from government yet essential to it in the total process of achieving the good life.

The theory finds clear and felicitous expression in the Massachusetts Constitution of 1780, whose chief architect and draftsman was John Adams. While guaranteeing the right of citizens to worship according to the dictates of their own consciences, the Constitution pointedly recognizes that "the happiness of a people and the good order and preservation of civil government essentially depend upon piety, religion, and morality" and that "these cannot be generally diffused through a community but by the institution of the public worship of God." It provides for education as follows:

> Wisdom and knowledge, as well as virtue, diffused generally among the body of the people, being necessary for the preservation of their rights and liberties . . . it shall be the duty of legislators and magistrates, in all future periods of this commonwealth, to cherish the interests of literature and the sciences, and all seminaries of them; especially the university at Cambridge, public schools and grammar schools in the towns; to encourage private societies and public institutions . . . ; to countenance and inculcate the principles of humanity and general benevolence, public and private charity, industry and frugality, honesty . . . sincerity, good humor, and all social affections and generous sentiments among the people.

Here clearly was another separation of powers in which raw material that could be protected and perhaps kept alive but could not be refined by government was to be refined by means appropriate to the task. Here, sketched out in John Adams' homely phrases, were the realm of the spirit and the realm of the mind, over which government could exercise sovereignty in only two ways, either as tyrant or as bungler. In either of these ways the cost to society would be the good life and, inevitably, free government. And if the good life and free government should be lost at home, of what avail our efforts against their enemies abroad?

This twofold separation of powers that was held so vital to our country by its founders has lost none of its vitality in a hundred and fifty years. It remains the "sacred maxim of free government," the *sine qua non* of the good life. But if the principle itself is clear, its application is subtle. It is easily overlooked, or cried down, in our hurry to get things done, especially in our anxious preoccupation with the tyranny that bestrides our world and threatens our freedom. It has to be carefully disentangled from business at hand, however urgent, and held as a measure against laws and policies, however meet.

This does not make it easy to invoke our principle. Amid the passions of the hour he who does so may be fiercely challenged. If he is, what authority can he cite, what intellectual and moral company shall he say he keeps? He can cite the "Records of the Federal Convention" of 1787, the Constitution of the United States, the *Federalist* papers, and the correspondence of John Adams and Thomas Jefferson. He can cite the *Politics* of Aristotle and *Two Treatises of Government* by John Locke. He can cite the Gospels according to Matthew, Mark, and Luke. And he can say that he has been keeping company with the authors of these works.

There are certain things that we can accomplish by law and there are certain things that we cannot accomplish by law or by any process of government. We cannot legislate intelligence. We cannot legislate morality. Nor can we legislate loyalty, for loyalty is a kind of morality. We cannot produce these things by decrees or commissions or public inquisitions.

Wisdom of this kind is born in man. It is awakened in

him by the fear of God. It is cultivated in him and through him put to the uses of society by true religion and liberal education. What was John Adams' charge to the government of Massachusetts? It was not that the government should take it upon itself to organize and manage this process but that the government should respect and give all possible support and encouragement to the schools and colleges and churches whose proper function that was.

There are certain things in man that have to be won, not forced; inspired, not compelled. Among these are many, I should say most, of the things that constitute the good life. All are essential to democracy. All are proof against its enemies.

Freedom, Security, and
the University Tradition

It is fitting that this theme should begin with a word of greeting to Columbia University in her bicentennial year from the alma mater of her first president, Samuel Johnson, a graduate of Yale in the class of 1714. It was not unusual in those days for dissatisfaction with one college to lead to the founding of another. I do not know that this motive played any such part in the founding of Columbia as it appears to have played in the founding of Yale; but if it did, I think we may now celebrate it as a healthy growing pain in a tradition that has conferred great benefits upon our civilization and is today nearing the ripe old age of a millennium. From the founding of Salerno to the two-hundredth anniversary of Columbia is a good thousand years, and from the founding of the two English universities from which both Columbia and Yale are directly descended nearly eight hundred.

These have not been years of contemplation. They have been years of mortal life, full of passions inimical to learning, innocent of its purposes, and hostile to its institutions. The university tradition has survived them all. That it has done so should give us courage who are entrusted with its welfare today; and for the part she has played in bringing that tradition to its present strength and prospects Yale salutes King's College and Columbia University.

It is fitting, too, that we should celebrate this occasion in the name of freedom. For what earth, air, fire, and water are to animate nature, freedom is to learning. A mind unfree, a mind possessed, dragooned, or indoctrinated, does not learn. It copies. Learning implies discovery. The unfree mind looks at maps but does not travel. It dares not. For at the edge of the maps is the jumping-off place, full of dragons and sea serpents. The unfree mind stays home, locks the door, bars the shutters. It is a hero in a crowd, a coward in solitude; it is a slave and a sloth. "High-day, freedom" sings the boozy Caliban in Shakespeare's *Tempest* as he indentures himself to new-found masters, "I'll kiss thy foot!" And then, at the end of the play:

> I'll be wise hereafter
> And seek for grace! What a thrice-double ass
> Was I to take this drunkard for a god,
> And worship this dull fool!

Caliban recapitulates much human history. The unfree mind is perpetually gulled, systematically swindled, periodically disillusioned. At all stages of the process it is the stuff that tyranny is made of. The unfree mind founded no universities, wrote no Declaration of Independence. It built the pyramids. It went on sprees and suffered remorse. Its principal contribution to humanity has been to remind us, at times all too forcibly, of our simian past.

It is easy to say what freedom is not. But what is it? Only concrete realization can give it objective meaning or existence. Freedom as Utopia is a pipe dream. Freedom as the future reward for present enslavement is a calculated fraud. Freedom with its head under the covers or talking in whispers is a travesty. The only definition of freedom that is worth anything to mankind is a concrete one—one that finds direct expression both in principle and in practice; in laws and the way those laws are enforced; in institutions and the uses to which those institutions are put; in policies and the methods by which those policies are conducted. For this reason the process of defining freedom is never finished. It must continue endlessly or there will be no freedom.

This should give us cause for concern. Though we celebrate freedom here tonight, over a large part of the earth the concrete definition of it has utterly ceased and in our part it has slowed almost to a standstill. Why so? On the other side of the iron curtain the reason is obvious. But at home? Why should the life process of freedom falter among its creators? Partly because we fear and mistrust our enemies and must devote so much energy to protecting ourselves against them. Partly because we fear and mistrust ourselves and choose to devote so much energy to catechizing one another. We are disposed to regard our times and circumstances as unprecedented in history and to see compelling reasons for suspending the definition of freedom in face of the needs of security and national defense.

There are two fundamental errors in this judgment. The first is the notion that our times and circumstances are unique. The second is the belief that defining freedom is incompatible with national security and defense. History is full of examples of freedom struggling for and finding concrete expression in times like ours. Nor is the difference between those times and our own to be found in the awesome text of nuclear physics. The Black Death in 1347 killed three quarters of the population of Europe. The Thirty Years' War (1618–48) reduced the population of Germany by more than a third, some historians say a half. Famine, with sudden and unexpected onset, malaria with endemic persistence, have reaped such a toll of human lives as would take the worst of nuclear weapons to equal. Plague and pestilence; battle, murder, and sudden death have haunted the human race from time immemorial, in forms as cruel and terrifying as hydrogen or cobalt. Fear seems to have been implanted in us, as it is in animals, for the self-preservation of the species. No sooner do we conquer it in one form than it is upon us in another; the forms change, but not the substance. If the definition of freedom had had to wait upon the perfection of security and defense measures in times gone by, the chances are there would be no freedom to talk about here tonight, and for that matter, no Yale and no Columbia.

Indeed, as we follow the history of modern democracy from its inception in the English revolutions of the seventeenth century to its culmination in the American Revolution and the Constitution of the United States, it would seem that the definers of freedom knew no times other than those of insecurity and war. In the seventeenth century, while Catholic power waxed and waned with the Thirty Years' War, then grew steadily stronger and more menacing with the rising power of France, English political life was deranged by fears much like our fear of communism today.

It became virtually impossible to carry on public discussion of any major question without evoking charges of subversion and treason on both sides. Pamphleteering plumbed the depths of diatribe. Accusations gained the force of convictions. Bills of attainder, star chamber, and impeachment proceedings filled the Tower of London. Differences of opinion ended in the pillory or on the scaffold. In 1634 Archbishop Laud condemned the Puritan lawyer and playwright Prynne to life imprisonment, a £5,000 fine, disbarment, and the loss of both his university degrees and his ears. Ten years later Prynne had his revenge, whipping up a hue and cry that sent Laud to the Tower and thence to the block. Milton's tutor at St. Paul's was sentenced to have his ears lopped off for drinking a sarcastic toast to the murderer of an imcompetent general in royal favor. Both Protectorate and Monarchy sent Lilburne to jail, as one beheaded the king and the other the regicides. At length, in the 1670's, with both Charles II and his Whig adversaries taking money from the King of France, English political morality had sunk to its lowest depths and with it the security of the realm.

Yet it was out of these times and circumstances that came the classic definitions of freedom which form the basis of modern democracy; and it was these definitions that brought security as well as justice to England. The essays of Bacon and Milton, the "Debates of the Army at Putney and Whitehall" (a little-known colloquy on the meaning of free government, as significant to the twentieth century as it was to the seventeenth), John Locke's *Of Civil Government,* and finally the Bill of Rights (1689) brought freedom down to earth and planted it firmly in a rule of law. This produced security and strength that no amount of hounding and hunting, of ear-lopping and head-chopping, had been able to produce.

The moral is plain. Cromwell perceived it, though imperfectly, in the midst of the wars when he said he would "rather have a plain russet-coated captain that knows what he fights for and loves what he knows, than what you call 'a gentleman' and is nothing else." Ireton sharpened Cromwell's perception when he declared in the Putney debates, "I will tell you what the soldier of this realm hath fought for: . . . the danger that we stood in was that one man's will must be a law. . . . There is no other foundation of right I know . . . but this general justice, and this general ground of righteousness, that we should keep covenant with one another." The perception was deepened a century and a half later by a graduate of King's College, Alexander

Hamilton, whose words are preserved in the Records of the Federal Convention, under the date of June 6, 1787: "A free government to be preferred to an absolute monarchy not because of the occasional violations of *liberty* or *property* but because of the tendency of the Free Government to interest the passions of the community in its favour, beget public spirit and public confidence."

The moral is this: that the surest safeguard against treason is a polity so just and equitable that no one will wish to betray it. Such an inspiration of men's affection and men's confidence is a more dependable guarantee of national security than the most searching catechism or the most diligent secret police. As we depart from this principle we confess our weakness, to our enemies as well as to ourselves. As we are faithful to it we realize our strength and show it to the world.

Which is the greater risk, that in translating the principles of a free society into public policy some false idea of freedom may slip into the translation, or that by suspending the process we turn ourselves into a whited sepulcher surrounded by detectives and supernatural weapons? There was risk in Milton's time, and in Locke's and Alexander Hamilton's. All sorts of political philosophy competed for their attention from the communism and totalitarianism of Plato and Hobbes to the paper paradises and dream worlds of More and Rousseau, each touting its wares in the name of freedom. Yet the founders of democracy were not deceived. They were no Calibans, nor overspecialized specialists nor inquisitors nor dialecticians. They were liberally educated men with both the wit and the learning to tell true freedom from false, undeceived by despotism because they knew at first hand the devious workings of one man's will, unterrified by it because they knew what they fought for and loved what they knew. Milton spoke for all of them when he said, "To sequester out of the world into Atlantic or Utopian polities, which never can be drawn into use, will not mend our conditions; but to ordain wisely in this world of evil, in the midst whereof God hath placed us unavoidably." And Benjamin Franklin summed up their achievement when he declared of the newly drafted Constitution of the United States, "It . . . astonishes me, sir, to find this system approaching so near to perfection as it does; and I think it will astonish our enemies, who are waiting with confidence to hear that our councils are confounded like those of the builders of Babel." The spirit and standards of these men are ours by national inheritance.

Two things in particular enabled them to ordain wisely in this world of evil: liberal learning and due process of law. These, too, are ours by inheritance. Liberal learning is both a safeguard against false ideas of freedom and a source of true ones. Due process of law provides an orderly framework within which the definition of freedom may be carried on without fear of subversion by one man's will, by enemy agents, or by popular hue and cry. Liberal learning and due process of law are root and branch of the university tradition. By putting them to such practical use in their day the English and American founders of democracy greatly strengthened that tradition. By putting them to the same use in our day we shall give that tradition a new lease on life. In the name of this high purpose I welcome Columbia to the third of many centuries.

The Cost of Freedom

The last word on freedom will never be spoken. Deeds, rather than words, are its most eloquent testimonial. We shall never complete our definition of freedom because, while we recognize it objectively as the absence of restraint, its truest meaning must always be subjective. We speak of the Four Freedoms as basic, yet we soon increase their number. Even among the four there is imperfect consistency, two being positive affirmations of things to enjoy (freedom of speech, freedom of religion) and two negative safeguards against things to avoid (freedom from want, freedom from fear). Between its sensible limits of servitude and license we find freedom as individuals in many forms. I do not intend to lecture on the meaning of a word that is sacred to all of us, both as American citizens and as members of the teaching profession. I shall assume, rather, the general meaning with which, through our laws and customs, we have invested the simple absence of restraint and offer, for what they are worth, a few thoughts which I hope may bring that meaning into sharper focus and its fulfillment within easier range.

Let me first dispose of a particular meaning of freedom that seems to have gained currency in the United States. This is the one that puts its stress on the first syllable of the word and identifies the whole word as a gratuity, as something available to anyone who desires it without payment or cost. With so many of the necessities of life now supplied on such terms, especially in the broad fields of health, education, and welfare, it is not surprising that freedom should be implicitly included among them. Yet there could be no more illusory commodity than free freedom. To assume its existence, as many of us do, is to assume an attitude that invites true freedom's destruction and demise.

We are all familiar with the adage that tells us that the price of liberty is eternal vigilance. This is the minimum price. As the Hungarians can testify and the pages of history confirm, freedom has always been one of the most costly of man's wants. To him who is denied it, through involuntary servitude or any other device, it is a priceless objective. To him who enjoys it, it is a priceless possession, one whose original value does not depreciate with age or use. But between what we might call kinetic freedom and potential freedom, there is this difference: kinetic freedom, however valuable, is not an end in itself. Once we have won it, it is no longer the mere fact or condition of freedom that counts, but the uses to which we put it. We may expand the four freedoms many times but we can find no room for such as freedom of idleness or freedom of ignorance. In this direction freedom soon loses itself in license. Or it destroys itself in subjective interpretations that violate the basic rule against restraint and turn one man's meat into another man's poison. It is within these outer limits that freedom offers its great benefits to man, provided he has the wit to perceive the limits; and provided, further, he has the enterprise to cultivate and improve such freedom as is vouchsafed to him by the society and circumstances in which he lives.

This choice and realization of uses imposes upon us a subtle economy of freedom, in which, as in all economies, we exchange goods and services for goods and services, toil and effort for value received. Just as the initial cost of freedom may range all the way from the mere attainment of citizenship to the supreme sacrifice of life itself, so the cost of maintaining it may vary; but it is never cheap. Vigilance is not enough: it can serve tyrants as well as the defenders of freedom. In the service of freedom, it is imperative that we know what to be vigilant about. The times read us a stern object lesson in this regard. During the past decade we in the United States have experienced our share of a world-wide conspiracy to destroy freedom, as a matter of principle. This conspiracy has been thwarted, and in the thwarting, vigilance has played an important part. Yet when the historical judgment of this experience is rendered, I fear it will be as a net loss to freedom rather than as a net gain. The effort to destroy freedom was countered by an effort to save it by reducing its scope.

The reason why vigilance thus miscarried is plain. Much of it was uninformed vigilance: the watchful eye in the empty head. It saw, or thought it saw, one enemy, shouted the alarm, and rushed all its forces into the fray, heedless of its tactics and neglectful of its defenses on other fronts. Its identification of the original enemy was correct. But through the uncritical use of tactics it sometimes honored that enemy by imitation and gave credence to the most abhorrent of enemy doctrines, namely that the end justifies the means. For example, while it deplored the hue and cry as employed by the enemies of freedom, it justified its use on the part of its defenders; it identified committee investigations with jury trials; it confused due process of law with legalistic pantomime. All of these practices were justified by the doctrine of present danger, with its overtone of *silent leges inter arma;* yet all left freedom apologizing for its reversion to primitive and incompatible ways, accusing itself by excusing itself, and morally weaker in the bargain.

Meanwhile, by allowing itself to become committed to

one enemy to the point of obsession, freedom allowed other enemies to gain ground, enemies such as ignorance, and the pervasive spirit of monopoly that curtails and restricts freedom in so many phases of our social and economic life. Ignorance is the arch enemy of freedom; by neglecting our schools we have given it a new lease on life. Beginning with business in the last century, the tendency toward bigness, centralization and regimentation has spread to government, labor, and agriculture. The mass media of radio and television impart a dreary sameness and a potentially dangerous uniformity to our cultural life. Organization, with its plethora of conferences and committees, its habitual delegation—therefore evasion—of responsibility and initiative, has become the order of the day. Though empirical in nature and avowedly innocent of the design, these trends, if allowed to proceed without reference to our basic principles of freedom, could result in a *de facto* totalitarianism hardly preferable to the one we oppose *de jure*. My point is that none of this was necessary, none of it need have happened, if vigilance had been properly informed.

This is particularly true of the freedom we claim for our profession, academic freedom. Of all types of freedom this is the least well understood. In the eyes of our profession it is nothing more than the application to academic circumstances of the civil liberties guaranteed by the Constitution of the United States. In the eyes of much of the public it is a special privilege of esoteric purpose and dubious validity presumably granted to teachers in partial substitution for more adequate compensation. When academic freedom came under attack, as it did, its defenders had to work under a severe handicap of obscurity. For this they had themselves very largely to blame. The plain fact was that for the most part their institutions had failed to instruct their own graduates in the elementary meaning and purposes of academic freedom, and lacking this instruction these graduates not only failed to understand it themselves but were unable to interpret it to the public. Nor was this accomplished by litigation: the law proved itself a better debater than it was a teacher. It, too, suffered from the general failure, especially regrettable in its own schools and the universities in which they were situated, to instruct the lay public in its own basic principles and purposes. A great unfinished task of education has yet to be completed before academic freedom will be secure. Vigilance is on guard, but vigilance needs the help of the teacher more than the lawyer.

The information of vigilance is the prime responsibility of education. So it was designated by the founders of the republic and so it remains today. Part of the true cost of freedom, in many respects superior in importance to national defense, is the maintenance of an educational system equal to this responsibility. If freedom has suffered from uninformed vigilance, it is because we have not been willing to pay that price. We must pay it or risk the loss of our freedom.

At the mention of educational costs a gloomy landscape· of deficits, shortages, and depressed salaries swims before our eyes. We have looked out upon this landscape now for the better part of a decade, shuddering at it, but doing little to improve it. Our excuse is that we cannot afford to do better. This is only an excuse, and a poor one. According to estimates supplied by the United States Office of Education, our total current plus capital expenditures on education for the year 1955–56 amounted to 15.5 billion dollars or 4 per cent of our gross national product for 1955, which was 390.9 billion dollars. Another computation shows current outlays on education not including capital expenditures to have comprised 4.7 per cent of our personal consumption expenditures, in which category it compares with certain other selected items as follows:

Item		Billions
Education		12.0
Elementary and secondary education	9.4	
Higher education	2.6	
Tobacco products and alcoholic beverages		14.5
New and used cars		14.4
Recreation		13.0

In the cold light of these figures, which could be amplified by our expenditures on such items as radio and television sets, cosmetics, toys, and sporting goods, what becomes of the argument that we cannot afford to do better by our educational system? There is nothing left of it. The figures show that we could allocate to education a substantially larger proportion of our wealth without depriving ourselves of necessities, without greatly denying ourselves pleasures—even luxuries—and without touching such crucial items in the national budget as health, social security, or defense. Our only valid reason for not doing so is that we do not wish to, not that the resources are lacking; and the most generous explanation of this lack of motive is lack of understanding. We have no trouble recognizing the cost of national security as part of the cost of our freedom and, on the strength of that recognition, in allocating to it a much larger share (10.5 per cent) of our gross national product. Once we saw them in the same light the needs of education would be met as promptly and as adequately as those of national security. Nor would such educational allocations be pure out-of-pocket expenses. Since they would be invested in the conservation and development of the country's most valuable natural resources, its human resources, they would constitute capital formation of the most fundamental kind.

But I am preaching to the converted. The country as a whole does not see the case as I have presented it. The statistics have received nation-wide publicity and attention. Yet they have not produced the necessary educational funds. They have been shouted from the housetops, but they have not generated the will to supply those funds. Could it be that there is something within our educational system, some inherent weakness, that makes it a faltering advocate in its own cause?

I suggest that there is. I suggest that by neglecting the liberal arts it has allowed its identity with freedom to become blurred and made it difficult for itself to represent this to the public. The widespread prevalence of vocational studies throughout our educational system is a not unnatural outgrowth of American history. It is rooted in our philosophy of education which, from the outset, prescribed such training for all citizens who desired it. But neither the facts of our history nor the philosophy that gives them life support such training as a substitute for the liberal arts. On the contrary, as every student of the lives and writings of the founders of our country knows, the liberal arts were considered to be the driving, motivating force of the whole educational system, through which each citizen was encouraged to progress as far and as fast as his native abilities permitted. In truth, those lives and writings proclaim the liberal arts as the educational source of the concepts of freedom embodied in the Constitution and the whole political philosophy of which it is the center.

The inhibiting weakness of our educational system today is that it has not faithfully adhered to that philosophy. It has produced virtually unlimited opportunities for training in the vocational skills required by our complex society but inadequate opportunities for contemplation of the meaning and purpose of those skills. It has at times lost sight of bona fide vocational training in the welter of hobbies, pastimes, and other activities that have managed to find a place in its curriculum. It has allowed those studies which for centuries have been esteemed and sought after as the intellectual and spiritual sustenance of free men and as the inspiration of a free society to become confused with other studies which, though useful in themselves, serve no such exalted—and essential—purpose, and to decline to a point well below their proper position in its curriculum. A recent study shows that the proportion of college and university students majoring in the liberal arts and sciences dropped from 43 per cent of the graduating class in 1940 to 35.7 per cent in 1952. Among male students graduating in 1955 the proportion was 26 per cent, and even this was heavily weighted with preprofessional studies having vocational purpose if not specific content. This is not to imply that the young men and women engaged in vocational studies care any less for freedom than the minority of their classmates enrolled in the liberal arts. It is to say that, at their best, vocational studies offer no such instruction in the meaning of freedom, such systematic testing and proving of freedom's basic principles, as the liberal arts do; while at their worst, vocational studies induce a kind of neutralism, a passive tendency to accept things as they are and conform to them, that is dangerous to freedom.

With our schools and colleges thus turning away from the classic image and inspiration of freedom, it is no wonder they have had trouble explaining freedom to the public or commending their interests in the name of freedom to the public's support. If they wish these things, they must reverse this trend. They must restore the liberal arts to

146

their rightful proportions in our educational system. This is the final and decisive item in this estimate of freedom's costs. It is the touchstone. We will spend enough on freedom to protect ourselves from enemy attack. We will spend enough on education to keep our children off the streets. But we shall not purchase true freedom at this price. For that we must pay extra, and for the will to do so that will supply the wealth, we must restore to good health and good repute the arts becoming free men.

The Colleges and
the Loyalty Oath

A debate of large dimensions is going on over the issue whether loyalty oaths and affidavits shall be required of college students seeking Federal loans. But the central issue is not always entirely clear to those directly involved, and is blurred and confused in the public mind. It is not a question of being for or against the Constitution, for or against loyalty. It is a case of two different groups of Americans talking at cross purposes about the same thing—namely, the security and welfare of the nation and the means of strengthening both through higher education. These are the only terms in which the central issue of the controversy can be accurately identified and understood.

Since the National Defense Education Act went into effect a year ago last September, the great majority of the nation's colleges and universities have raised their voices in criticism of one particular provision. This is the disclaimer affidavit that accompanies the oath of allegiance, and that is required of all recipients of the Act's benefits. The affidavit requirement appears in Title X, Section 1001 (f), the full text of which reads as follows:

> No part of any funds appropriated or otherwise made available for expenditure under authority of this Act shall be used to make payments or loans to any individ-

ual unless such individual (1) *has executed and filed with the Commissioner an affidavit that he does not believe in, and is not a member of and does not support any organization that believes in or teaches, the overthrow of the United States Government by force or violence or by any illegal or unconstitutional methods,* and (2) has taken and subscribed to an oath or affirmation in the following form: "I do solemnly swear (or affirm) that I will bear true faith and allegiance to the United States of America and will support and defend the Constitution and laws of the United States against all its enemies, foreign and domestic." The provisions of section 1001 of title 18, United States Code, shall be applicable with respect to such affidavits.

Individually, and through such representative organizations as the Association of American Colleges, the Association of American Universities, the American Association of Land Grant Colleges and State Universities, the American Association of University Professors, and the Association for Higher Education of the National Education Association, the colleges and universities have protested this affidavit and have urged its repeal.

The Government has not been unresponsive to their views. Last winter the Secretary of Health, Education and Welfare, Mr. Flemming, testified in their support, and Senators Clark of Pennsylvania and Kennedy of Massachusetts introduced a bill repealing Section 1001 (f) in its entirety. Hearings on this bill, which had the approval of the Department of Health, Education and Welfare, were held before the Senate Committee on Labor and Public Welfare in April and May, and the committee reported the bill favorably by a vote of 12 to 3.

After debate in late July, however, the bill was amended to

eliminate the disclaimer affidavit but retain the oath of allegiance, and then sent back to committee. Finally, on December 2, on the eve of his departure for his trip abroad, President Eisenhower spoke out categorically in favor of the affidavit's repeal. There the matter rests awaiting reconsideration by Congress when it assembles next month.

The colleges and universities are not protesting the oath of allegiance. They do question its appropriateness as a condition to financial aid for college students, as distinct from its traditional usage in connection with the assumption of a public office or trust; and they also question whether more general use may not wear it thin.

Too, they are mindful of the historic fact that any oath required by the state can be misused. Nevertheless, they accept the oath of allegiance. By itself the oath is no more than an affirmation of the duties every citizen owes to his country, whether he takes the oath or not. It is thus co-extensive with and expressive of the basic law of the land. The disclaimer affidavit, on the other hand, extends beyond the basic law of the land into the realm of belief and conscience, where definitions are vague and actions become matters of debate. What the colleges and universities are objecting to is this disclaimer affidavit.

Unfortunately, these are not the terms in which the issue is commonly presented. Although the position of the colleges and universities is extensively documented in the printed hearings on the Clark-Kennedy bill and in the Congressional Record, and has attracted widespread press attention, what comes through to the public is an oversimplified impression of fastidious intellectualism finding fault with the law, of the egghead refusing to accept the common lot of the citizen and the patriot.

What's wrong with loyalty oaths? We have all pledged allegiance to the flag as school children. Everyone who takes out a passport swears to uphold the Constitution. Why should anyone hesitate to take such an oath in any circumstances? Why should any American object to disclaiming beliefs abhorrent to all Americans? These and less temperate questions imputing subversiveness and disloyalty are evidence of a wide gulf of misunderstanding between the public and the colleges and universities.

A natural reason for the position of the colleges and universities is that no one enjoys being doubted when everyone else is trusted. Yet this is the way the colleges and universities are made to feel by the disclaimer affidavit. The affidavit originated in the Taft-Hartley Act. From this Act it was written into the National Science Foundation Act of 1950, and then into the National Defense Education Act of 1958. Farmers, veterans, and beneficiaries of social security (to say nothing of other recipients of Federal benefits, such as the officials and employees of railroads, steamship lines, and airlines) have never had to make a disclaimer affidavit. In 1959 it was dropped out of the Taft-Hartley Act. This means that the only recipients of Federal benefits to whom it now applies are students and teachers in colleges and universities.

To the latter, this seems like the short end of the stick. They do not see why their students and faculties should be treated differently from any other individuals, groups, professions, or occupations that receive Federal subsidies or loans. And it is all the harder for them to appreciate the justice of this when they reflect on the role they are being asked to perform and the manner in which they are being asked to perform it. In one and the same breath they are told that they are the nation's first line of defense—and the nation's poorest security risk. They are called upon to put forth their best effort in the name of national security; yet they alone are obliged to submit to certain qualifications concerning their loyalty.

To them, this seems worse than discrimination in the ordinary sense of the word. It seems like a vote of no confidence from the very party that is asking them to come to its aid, at the very moment and in the very circumstances in which that aid is most urgently needed.

Is this the result of a native anti-intellectualism that stubbornly survives even the most serious crises? Whatever its origin, the fact is that the most important Act of Congress to identify education with the national interest since the Land Ordinance of 1785 and the Morrill Act of 1862 singles out higher education from all professions and occupations as a dubious loyalty risk—which goes far to explain the objections of the colleges and universities.

Feeling as they do, the colleges and universities are all the more averse to being parties to the discriminatory practice. Yet this, too, is forced upon them by the terms of the National Defense Education Act. In the student loan program the institution is required to invest 10 per cent of its own funds in each loan, and to administer the disclaimer affidavit and oath of allegiance to each recipient.

Thus the institution not only becomes an active agent in administering an affidavit of which it does not approve; it also is forced to adopt a double standard for its students, as only those who need financial assistance are required to take the affidavit and oath. This places the institution in a moral dilemma which none enjoys, and which a number have decided they could resolve only by refraining from or withdrawing from participation in the loan program.

It is true that repeal of the affidavit will not wholly relieve the colleges and universities of the discriminatory practices of which they complain. Students and faculty accepting benefits under the terms of the National Defense Education Act will, presumably, still be required to take the oath of allegiance, while others will not. But, as already pointed out, the colleges and universities regard the oath of allegiance as a far less onerous requirement than the disclaimer affidavit, and one that, in present circumstances, is supportable.

Another and purely practical reason for the objection of the colleges and universities to the disclaimer affidavit is their belief that it is inherently futile. They know that similar affidavits have led to some convictions for perjury. But they do not think the affidavit can be relied upon either as a safeguard against disloyalty or as a means of inculcating loyalty.

That no truly subversive or treasonous person would hesitate to use it—or the oath of allegiance, for that matter—as a cloak for his intentions has been proved, rather than disproved, by the perjury convictions.

On the other hand, the affidavit cannot create loyalty. Loyalty cannot be coerced or compelled. If men are born loyal, the only kind of loyalty that survives infancy in any thinking person is the kind that survives curiosity and withstands criticism and even doubt. Such loyalty may and usually does have an instinctive base; but if the opportunity to satisfy curiosity and answer criticism is limited, or qualified, or made conditional upon the acceptance of restraints, the instinctive base of loyalty is undermined.

The only loyalty upon which true reliance can be placed is the kind evoked by the inherent virtue of the cause or institution or individual toward which the loyalty is felt. In creating this kind of loyalty, oaths of any sort are of little value compared to the devotion of a man who has been free to examine and evaluate the evidence and, on the strength of that experience, in Cromwell's words, "knows what he fights for and loves what he knows."

While the oath of allegiance may have the effect of recalling or stimulating such a sense of loyalty in the person who takes it, that effect is hardly strengthened by the accompanying affidavit. When a man pledges his allegiance to the Government and the Constitution, either we take him at his word (in which case the disclaimer affidavit becomes tautological) or we doubt his word and say to him (as the affidavit seems to say), "Even though you have just affirmed your allegiance to the Government and the Constitution, you are still not to be trusted." In the latter case the affidavit implies perjury in taking the oath of allegiance. In either case it is difficult for the colleges and universities to see how it will inspire loyalty in the rising generation.

The question now presents itself, why are the colleges and universities objecting to the affidavit in the National Defense Education Act, when for nearly a decade they have acquiesced in it in the National Science Foundation Act?

The answer is that, although they have not liked it in either Act, in the National Science Foundation Act the affidavit was the responsibility of the individual receiving the benefit. But in the National Defense Education Act, through investment in the loan program and administration of the affidavit, the institution itself is involved.

Again, the broader scope of the National Defense Education Act, its trail-blazing character, and its weightier impact on the younger generation make the affidavit stand out more prominently as a matter of principle. It was also felt that the National Defense Education Act might be establishing the pattern for Federal support of higher education and setting the example for governmental relations with the colleges and universities for the indefinite future; and in this context matters of principle assumed special importance. When the framers of the National Defense Education Act followed the precedent of the Taft-Hartley and National Science Foundation Acts, and the disclaimer affidavit seemed about to be frozen into the system, the colleges and universities decided the time had come to make their opposition known.

But the case of the colleges and universities rests on more than mere discomfort at being objects of and parties to discriminatory practices. One possible remedy for any such practice is to generalize it. If every recipient of Federal benefits and all students in higher education were required to make the affidavit, the colleges and universities could no longer plead that they were suffering from discrimination.

The truth is they would find this cure no better than the disease. Justice Holmes once said that questions like this were better answered by a page of history than a volume of logic. The fundamental position of the colleges and universities is rooted in history, and it is only through an understanding of that history that we can fully understand what they are driving at today. The gravamen of their case against the affidavit is that, in juxtaposition to the affirmative oath of allegiance, it distorts the combination and imbues it with the nature of a political test oath.

This is the historic way in which such oaths have been constructed. They invariably begin with simple declarations or affirmations of allegiance, like the ancient oath of fealty or the present oath of allegiance. They are then expanded (as by the disclaimer affidavit) to include more and more avowals or disavowals of beliefs, doctrines, and associations, as well as denials of unpopular or criminal acts. Thus they project the authority of the state into the realm of belief and conscience where, according to our political tradition, it has no business; and the individual may be forced to acquit himself of crimes and offenses left so vague that he can be convicted on the mere appearance of evil if he cannot be convicted of its practice.

Experience has taught us lessons about political and religious test oaths which are all too easily forgotten. It was under the scourge of these oaths that our Protestant ancestors emigrated from England to settle in America; that our Catholic ancestors lost their lands and lives; that Sir Thomas More died telling his daughter, "It was a very hard thing to compel me to say either precisely with it against my conscience to the loss of my soul, or precisely against it to the destruction of my body"; that Puritan dissenters and Quakers went to jail, sat in the stocks, and had their ears cut off.

The oaths that caused these sufferings grew to be over a page long, and, in the words of Sir Frederick Pollock, became "swollen with strange imprecations and scoldings," until in 1868 they were at last abolished in favor of the simple oath of allegiance.

"I,   do swear that I will be faithful and bear true allegiance to Her Majesty Queen Victoria, her heirs and successors, according to law. So help me God."

These things are easily forgotten, but colleges and universities, where history is studied and the past is ever present, remember them. They were fresh in the minds of the framers of our Constitution, fresh enough for Alexander Hamilton to denounce test oaths as "a subversion of one great principle of social security, to wit: That every man shall be presumed innocent until he is proved guilty."

Their effect, said Hamilton, "was to invert the order of things, and instead of obliging the state to prove the guilt, in order to inflict the penalty, it was to oblige the citizen to establish his own innocence to avoid the penalty. It was to excite scruples in the honest and conscientious, and to hold out a bribe to perjury." All this, Hamilton concluded, was "repugnant to the true genius of the common law" and "unknown to the Constitution . . . "

The colleges and universities recall more recent experiences with test oaths than those which began with the marital troubles of Henry VIII. They recall the oaths of religious conformity that bound the early American colleges in the eighteenth century and were not finally sloughed off until the nineteenth (by Oxford and Cambridge in the middle of the nineteenth)—oaths that militated against Catholics and Protestant sects dissenting from the established religion of the institution.

They recall, too, the loyalty oaths imposed by Congress in the Reconstruction period after the Civil War, of which Lincoln declared: "I have found that men who have not even been suspected of disloyalty are very averse to taking an oath of any sort as a condition to exercising an ordinary right of citizenship."

In the words of the Supreme Court (in *Ex Parte Garland*), "All enactments of this kind partake of the nature of bills of pains and penalties, and are subject to the constitutional inhibitions against the passage of bills of attainder, under which general designation they are included."

For the benefit of a generation which, fortunately for it, has less knowledge of them than the men who drafted the Constitution, bills of attainder were arbitrary bills which extinguished the civil rights of an individual and enabled the state to impose upon him such penalties as loss of property, prison and death, without benefit of trial by jury. Bills of attainder and test oaths grew up together in the same country, in the same period of history, and, although they are not identified with one another in modern law, they partook of the same essence in their day and served the same brand of justice.

That oaths of allegiance, even without the objectionable features of the historic test oaths, can be misused as instruments of oppression was proved by Hitler. He merely required that civil servants and professors swear allegiance to him. That was all he needed to give the semblance of legality to whatever coercive steps he chose to take to compel their adherence to the Nazi party line.

It was in no small measure his use of the oath that drove many German university professors into exile—among them many of the leading nuclear scientists who enabled the United States to produce the atomic bomb instead of Germany. They and their fellow-exiles in other fields of learning, finding posts in American universities, have testified to the dangers of all oaths, however innocuous their beginning, in a way that has undoubtedly made their American colleagues sensitive to those dangers.

The colleges and universities do not believe that the oath of allegiance in the National Defense Education Act will be used as Hitler used his oath of allegiance. Indeed, as I have already said, they have accepted it. But the German experience, with its peculiarly direct and intimate significance to our college and university community, and that community's continually fresh memory of the political and religious test oaths in Anglo-American history, make it that much more anxious lest the disclaimer affidavit bend the present oath of allegiance in the direction of either. Hence it is that much more critical of the affidavit and more strongly in favor of its repeal.

Underlying this concern with test oaths, in fact underlying the whole position of the colleges and universities in this controversy, is their concern for freedom. For centuries, in Europe as well as in England and America, they have struggled for the right to pursue learning for its own sake without interference by church or state. They have done so not because they thought society owed them this right as a mark of respect or a special privilege, but because they have regarded it as a functional necessity identical with freedom of the press and similar to freedom of speech, freedom of religion, and freedom of assembly.

158

In this historical perspective, they see a consistent use of oaths like the disclaimer affidavit as instruments of coercion, conformism and oppression, which are enemies of learning as much as they are opposites of freedom. If, now, our colleges and universities are to serve the cause of freedom and discharge the solemn duties with which the public, through the National Defense Education Act, has vested them, they can do so effectively only through procedures consistent with both freedom and learning.

Again and again history affords object lessons of what happens to learning when it is denied the freedom that is its natural medium. Nazi Germany is a glaring example. A nation that cannot trust its intellectuals cannot trust itself. A people that is afraid to expose its political and social institutions to the curiosity and criticism of the rising generation is not free; by whatever method it whispers this fear to itself, it shouts its insecurity to the world.

It is not the disclaimer affidavit that will make our colleges and universities bulwarks of our security, nor even the oath of allegiance, which they accept. It is our trust in them to pursue the course the nation has set for them—a course they can pursue in freedom and in no other way.

The Basis of a Rule of Law

Which is better, a government of men or a government of laws? If one has never attempted to answer that question, he has managed somehow to avoid the *pons asinorum* of political philosophy. "Give us good men and they will make us good Lawes is the Maxime of a Demagogue," says Milton's contemporary, James Harrington. "But give us good orders, and they will make us good men, is the Maxime of a Legislator, and the most infallible in the Politickes." The framers of our Constitution did not go quite so far as believing that good laws alone would make good men: they counted on religion and education for that. But they went as far as they could to provide the United States with a government forever secure against the passions of mobs and the ambitions of demagogues. Their solution to the *pons asinorum* was a government of laws.

American tradition echoes their conclusion, repeats it endlessly in all procedures by which we govern ourselves and manage our affairs. No philosopher kings or benevolent despots for us: they are too near cousins to tyrants. Sooner or later all bidders for such fame have discovered the strength of our tradition. Yet I submit that this question which appears to have only one answer confronts us with a choice more real to political philosophy than it is to politics; that we have in fact both a government of laws and a government of men; that each is essential to the other; and that our only real choice in the matter is whether or not—and by what means—to preserve their mutual welfare.

The importance of a government of laws to the individuals who live under it is obvious. Only such a government can, in the words of *The Federalist*, "obtain for rulers men who possess most wisdom to discern, and most virtue to pursue, the common good of society; and in the next place . . . take the most effectual precautions for keeping them virtuous whilst they continue to hold their public trust." Only such a government can ensure the maximum diffusion of opportunity and responsibility, of talent and virtue, through society. No such liberation of man's individual powers is possible where the whim of a despot prevails or the rules of caste or dialectic coop people up in cages and categories. Where all are equal under law and none can place himself above it, the individual achieves his greatest usefulness, as well as his greatest freedom.

The importance of a government of men to a government of laws is less obvious. For one thing, our *pons asinorum* leads to the assumption that the two are antithetical. For another much evil has come from governments of men, as it did, for example, from the despotisms of former times and as it has from the communist and fascist dictatorships of today. This experience has obscured the fact that, no matter how carefully defined and administered, no government of laws is insensible to what Plato termed "The endless irregular movements of human things." Laws are made by men, interpreted by men, and enforced by men, and in the continuous process, which we call government, there is continuous opportunity for the human will to assert itself. This is true even of the common law. With its slow, seemingly automatic accumulation of precedent, it may look to laymen like a coral reef. The legal philosopher knows it to be a finely wrought cathedral. "We know how much can be done by one man, acting and speaking only for himself, to build up a common law," writes Justice Cardozo. "Kent and Story did it in their day. . . . One dare not estimate the number of sane and sound judgments, useful members of society, that would have been brought into the world defective and deformed without the guidance of these masters." Such is the government of men that flourishes within the most perfect government of laws and embodies in itself powers of wreckage or redemption.

What restraints or influences are there to determine which character those powers will assume? In the final analysis, when all the answers reason gives are counted, there is only one, and that is morality. Though society all too often ignores this truth, the law itself repeatedly recognizes it. During the trials of Alger Hiss and recently, during the hearings of the Senate Permanent Subcommittee on Investigations in Washington, masses of evidence, feats of detection, dialectical skill, and procedural technicalities often yielded to considerations regarding the credibility of witnesses. Thus law acknowledged its dependence upon morality in one of its oldest and most elemental forms.

A corollary to the proposition comes from the experience of Ignazio Silone, the Italian novelist, a disillusioned ex-member of the Communist party and now one of its leading adversaries. Silone recalls a meeting of the Communist International in Moscow in the early 'twenties at which the Russian delegate put forward a suggestion which seemed as obvious to him as Columbus' egg.

"The branches," he suggested, "should declare that they submit to the discipline demanded, and then, in practice, should do exactly the contrary." The English

Communist interrupted, "But that would be a lie." Loud laughter greeted this ingenuous objection; frank, cordial, interminable laughter, the like of which the gloomy offices of the Communist International had perhaps never heard before. . . . The general hilarity gave the English Communist's timid, ingenuous objection its true meaning. And that is why, in my memory, the storm of laughter aroused by that short, almost childishly simple little expression—"But that would be a lie"—outweighs all the long, heavy oppressive speeches I heard during sittings of the Communist International, and has become a kind of symbol for me.

I draw another corollary from the experience of the atom spy Klaus Fuchs. When, after his conviction at the Old Bailey in March 1950, Fuchs was asked if he had anything to say, this is how he replied: "My Lord, I have committed certain crimes, for which I am charged, and I expect sentence. I have also committed some other crimes, which are not crimes in the eyes of the law—crimes against my friends; and when I asked my counsel to put certain facts before you, I did not do it because I wanted to lighten my sentence. I did it in order to atone for those other crimes." For nearly eighteen years Fuchs had led a double life as a member of the Communist party and an outstanding nuclear physicist. For nearly eight of those years, despite all security precautions—that is to say, all law as it applied to and governed his particular activities—he had deliberately and without the slighest qualms of conscience betrayed his country and his professional trust. He had come at last to live at the Harwell Atomic Energy Establishment in England, where, apparently for the first time in his life, he discovered the meaning of friendship. Whereupon, still unrestrained and unapprehended by law, he went to his security officer and of his own free will confessed his crimes. For Fuchs as for Silone a simple moral principle had become as the pebble of David that slew Goliath, a force more powerful and compelling than all the law which restrained and protected them from communism on the one hand or, in twisted logic, exacted their allegiance to it on the other.

But though law depends upon morality, it cannot by itself create or even guarantee that upon which it depends: individual moral integrity. If the devil can quote Scripture he can also cloak his activities in the habiliments of law. No systems of government have made a greater show of legalism than the communist and fascist dictatorships of recent date. Yet both rose to power by deliberately destroying the moral integrity of individuals, which they rightly regarded as an obstacle to their despotic practices and highly subjective uses of law. Defamation, intimidation, trumped-up evidence, and secret and ambiguous accusations are as familiar weapons in communist and fascist arsenals as brain washing and secret police. No matter where or in what cause such weapons are put to use, their result is always the same: to undermine the foundation of a government of laws.

What safeguards have we against such a development in the United States? There is a spirit abroad in the country that speaks of love in the accents of hate; that would fight fire with fire; that seeks whole truths in half truths and spreads accusations wholesale in hopes of convictions retail. The passions of men ever incline them in this direction. "So strong is this propensity of mankind to fall into mutual animosities," says *The Federalist* in its wisdom, "that where no substantial occasion presents itself, the most fanciful distinctions have been sufficient to kindle their unfriendly passions and excite their most violent conflicts." History has presented us with both a substantial occasion and fanciful distinctions. It has presented us with the substantial occasion of a world-wide conspiracy which we know from experience stops at nothing save our own strength in its efforts to accomplish our downfall; and from this terrifying prospect flow all manner of fanciful distinctions which have aroused our passions. Yet the end of passion's trail is chaos, the opportunity of the demagogue, the entering wedge of dictatorship, the military hope of our enemies. What assurances have we that any or all such evils will not overwhelm our government of laws?

We have, it is true, the Constitution and the Bill of Rights. Long before these were adopted, ancient laws of libel sought to prevent anonymous accusations of crime; to compel accusers to assume full responsibility for their accusations, to stand forth and prove their words; to put an end to appeals to passion, to private revenge and public tumult. These laws hark back to the Theodosian Code and weave their way in consistent pattern through the fabric of the common law. All such constitutional and legal provisions bespeak a tradition of great age and vitality. Yet in the last analysis we have no surer safeguard than the Ninth Commandment. For this Commandment guarantees the integrity of the government of men that sustains our government of laws.

Law is founded upon morality, and morality finds its foundation in the moral integrity of the individual. Destroy this and we destroy morality. Destroy morality and we destroy law. These consequences follow upon one another in government just as surely as the progressive debasement of a currency brings about the collapse of an economy.

> Thou shalt not bear false witness against thy neighbor. Thou shalt not raise a false report; put not thine hand with the wicked to be an unrighteous witness.

Thou shalt not follow a multitude to do evil; neither shalt thou speak in a cause to decline after many to wrest judgment.

Thus did Mosaic Law insist upon the truth, the whole truth, and nothing but the truth. Thus did it prohibit false or ambiguous accusations, the hue and cry, or any substitution of the will of the mob for due process of law. These provisions were not written into Mosaic Law for the mere accommodation of individuals. They were written into it in order that it might function as a system of government. All that they have meant to the Christian civilization founded upon that Law they continue to mean to our own government and civilization today; law and order, inner strength, and true external security.

Going to the Devil

There was a time when a sermon that began by asking the congregation what it thought about the devil or how it stood in relation to hell would not have seemed as startling as it might today. To the founders of our country and its educational system these were far from rhetorical questions. They were as real in essence and as practical in implication as any which a public opinion poll could put to us today. For in their day and age the devil was fully, not to say gainfully, employed, both on his own account and, paradoxically, in the interests of the church. In leading people astray and finding work for idle hands to do he was, of course, in business for himself. At the same time, as a kind of double agent, he worked for the church, scaring in converts and jacking up backsliders.

Whatever else can be said about the devil, he was versatile and he was industrious. As a cloven-hoofed monster he could frighten the wayward out of their waywardness (and sometimes out of their wits), were they puritan mystics in New England or turf-cutters on lonely Irish bogs. But as Hamlet observed, the devil also had power to assume a pleasing shape. As Satan in *Paradise Lost* he was the most beautiful of the angels fallen the lowest; as Mephistopheles he was a sophisticated colleague to the learned Faust. There was no limit to his repertoire or to the settings in which he could appear. His industry was prodigious. No union hours or coffee breaks for him. He was always at work, for himself at his evil, and for his foes at their virtue, recruiting his own legions of evildoers when he could, strengthening the ranks of the virtuous when he could not, the omnipresent, instantly available, readily understandable cause and explanation of moods, vapors, and misconduct in humans and of why things went wrong in human affairs.

Hell, too, was ever present in people's minds, elaborately described and mapped in topographical detail by artists and poets as well as by theologians. It was so near and real to the Connecticut clergy of the eighteenth century that sermons lasting two hours and continuing for several Sundays on such themes as *The Future Punishment of the Wicked Unavoidable and Intolerable,* and *The Eternity of Hell's Torments* were not uncommon. I have selected these titles from the works of the eminent Yale graduate Jonathan Edwards, whose career as theologian and leader of the great awakening in the Connecticut Valley was crowned by his appointment as President of Princeton.

Edwards's most famous sermon, a classic of its kind, was *Sinners in the Hands of an Angry God,* preached at Enfield, Connecticut, on July 8, 1741 and according to an early editor, "attended with remarkable impressions on many of the hearers." For this sermon Edwards chose the text I have borrowed from him this morning, "Their foot shall slide in due time." He did so, he told his congregation, because it implied not only that "he that walks in slippery places is every moment liable to fall" but also that most of his congregation stood on just such slippery ground and could expect to remain there only until the appointed time for God to let them fall off into the abyss that yawned at the edge of it. Meanwhile, he said, "The God that holds you over the pit of hell, much as one holds a spider, or some lothsome insect, over the fire, abhors you, and is dreadfully provoked; his wrath towards you burns like fire; he looks upon you as worthy of nothing else, but to be cast into the fire; . . . you are ten thousand times so abominable in his eyes, as the most hateful venomous serpent is in ours."

Once the fateful hour struck there could be no appeal for clemency, from the punishment that followed no deliverance: "you must wear out long ages, millions and millions of ages, in wrestling and conflicting with this merciless vengeance." It is not surprising that contemporaries should have attested to "remarkable impressions" on the part of Edwards's congregation. The impressions were vivid and terrifying, and their immediate effect was to impel many of the congregation to make personal decisions and commitments not only having to do with faith but resulting in actions and deeds.

When we compare our ways and attitudes with these it becomes obvious, does it not, that neither this devil nor this hell has survived modern scientific inquiry. Concerning this change two propositions suggest themselves. The first is that although we may gratify ourselves with the progress we have made through scientific inquiry it is also possible to look wistfully and perhaps with some regret upon the abandonment of some of the old ways.

Take the devil. Might he not still serve some useful purposes? Might it not, for instance, have been more satisfactory for us to have been able to hold him to account for rigging television quizzes than to have to accept the explanation that this was done, with the knowledge and approval of their chief participant—the member of a profession dedicated to learning and truth—as a means of inspiring in his audiences a love for learning and truth? Again, if the devil were back in circulation, would we have had so much trouble understanding the collapse of the Summit Conference in Paris a few years ago? We could simply have assumed that the devil had got hold of Khrushchev; or that Khrushchev was (or is) the devil—an assumption complicated only by the fact that some people believe Mao Tse-tung is the devil and others General Malinovsky.

In clarifying the U–2 affair the devil might have been very

helpful. In this case, he could either have ordered the flight or caused the plane's engine to fail (or both); and he certainly could have been responsible for the official explanations of the event that followed it. An alibi is a risky defense. If it is cracked, any alternative defense becomes difficult. If your position is that you were not at the scene of the crime when the crime was committed and the case begins to go against you, how then can you fall back on the argument that you did not mean to do it or that you did it in self-defense? Thus to explain that a plane was a weather plane, then that it was a reconnaissance plane that we did not know about, then that it was a reconnaissance plane that had got lost, then that it was not lost but was carrying out an essential mission, then that such missions would be continued, then that they would be stopped, sounds like the devil. Would it not have made life much simpler for us if we could have said that that was exactly who it was, the devil, adding opportunely to an already sizable collection of monkey wrenches of Russian manufacture for Khrushchev to throw into the machinery in Paris?

The regret we might feel over the fading away of Jonathan Edwards's hell under scientific inquiry might well be more poignant. One of the weaknesses in Edwards's delineation of hell was that no one had actually ever been there and seen it. To make up for this, Edwards had to employ all the rhetorical skill at his command and summon all the reserves of his own passionate faith in order to convince his congregation of the reality of the fiery lake which he said was burning and flaming beneath them.

We need neither rhetoric nor faith to convince us of the reality and the nearness of our hell. People have seen it with their own eyes. In the empirical knowledge of living scientists are certainties as dreadful as the most dreadful in Jonathan Edwards's imagination. Our hell is utterly real. There it lies, just beyond the range of our normal lives, out of sight but never out of mind. Another difference between our hell and Jonathan Edwards's is that from the latter, as even the grim Calvinist himself conceded, there was one certain escape. This was to embrace the Christian faith with whole heart and mind and cast oneself on the mercy of Christ. For us who hold that faith, since those who do not hold it have the power to open the gates of hell regardless of our actions, no escape seems certain. For this reason we might regret the passing of the puritan hell even more than we might the disappearance of the puritan devil.

This brings me to my second proposition regarding change and progress, namely, that although these have done away with the old devil and the old hell they have by no means done away with the problem of evil. Nor have they simplified that problem. The responsibility for distinguishing between good and evil and making the right choice between them rests as heavily upon us as it did upon our ancestors. In truth it rests more heavily. For one thing, we no longer have the devil to blame for our shortcomings: we have only ourselves. For another thing, we are more highly organized, both nationally and internationally, and therefore can do more harm to one another by making the wrong choice or more good by making the right one.

We feel the weight of this responsibility most when we think of our nuclear hell. Many a prayer is offered nowadays, and many a sermon preached, reminding us of our sins and shortcomings on the one hand and of the proximity of this hell on the other. Somehow or other they leave a gap between our personal sense of responsibility for the conduct of our own individual lives and the impersonal hell we have created for ourselves. Indeed, instead of instructing or inspiring us in our personal conduct, all representations and presentiments of this hell, no matter how awful, seem merely to stupefy us. They seem to drive us to quite a different escape from that which Jonathan Edwards held out to his congregation: to affected stoicism or escapism, in various ingeniously contrived and luxuriously appointed fools' paradises.

Is this the paralyzing effect of fear? Or is it evidence of the inadequacy of fear as a source of moral regeneration? Whatever it is, if we permit it to deaden our sense of responsibility for the way we lead our own lives, *our* foot is likely to slide in due time. It is this attitude more than any other single factor that menaces our society. It could defeat us before the Russians had fired a single missile. By appearing to give in to it, as we do now, we create a false impression of demoralization and decadence which might tempt our enemies into a desperate military gamble and so precipitate the universal disaster. By actually giving in to it, which might happen if we should allow present tendencies to become fixed habits, we should so greatly impair the standards and prospects of our civilization that its survival might become a matter of indifference even to its members.

As Aristotle said long ago, every society exists for some good. What is the good for which American society exists? That, above all others, is the question to which the whole world awaits an answer. How can any American citizen give it for his country unless he is first able to give it for himself?

We are not sinners in the hands of an angry God. We are not suspended in a surrealist half life where good and evil are all mixed up and nobody knows or cares which is which or who is responsible for either. We are citizens of a country whose character is a composite of our characters. It is by what we are and what we do that our country will be judged. These are eternal truths, made more compelling by the realities of our world than they were by the diabolical apparatus and imagery of our forefathers. By perceiving them and applying them to our own lives we will ensure that our foot shall not slide, with or without the good offices of the devil.

Society's Need for Man

The preparation of free men for life in a free society assumes the existence not only of a particular type of student but also of a particular set of conditions in which he will live and work. We were born free men. But when we speak of a free society, do we not beg the question? By what evidence do we judge the society into which we graduate our students to be free? I speak of freedom here not in the terms of Caliban or the noble savage, nor yet the rugged individualist of American fame, but as a *modus vivendi* that permits us to follow the devices and desires of our own hearts within Christian limits, that gives scope for the decent impulses of individuals, and makes it possible for free men to function as such. If these conditions do not exist, or if their existence is doomed, of what avail our principle of education?

The outlook is not encouraging. Quite apart from the clinical study of radioactive fall-out now in progress, which reduces us all to motes in the scientists' beam, and the cold war that generates such lethal heat, this is the age of organization. The cold war, with its emphasis upon national security; national security with its emphasis upon nuclear weapons; nuclear weapons with their emphasis upon methods of production that isolate and regiment the producers like the votaries of some secret religious cult—all this, and the fear of Armageddon that inspires it, impels us to organize to a degree heretofore undreamed of in this

173

land of the free. But these lurid, latter-day phenomena are only the latest—one dare not say the last—projection of a trend that began more than a hundred years ago. This was the reorganization of our economic life caused by the industrial revolution. The strategic organization now enjoined upon the country by the cold war merely caps the climax in the history of the great corporations, labor unions, agricultural producers' and marketers' associations, and myriad groups of similar nature, most of them with governmental shadows or counterparts, that characterize our economic society. By economic society I mean our human society in its working hours. Nor has our passion for organization spent itself in the economic sphere. Every thought and action, indeed every feeling of which we are capable as human beings, has found an organization of some sort purporting to strengthen and improve it by the process of division.

The prospect is enough to give pause to any man educated in the tradition of individual freedom. The whole purpose of such education is to awaken and develop the individual to the full limit of his intellectual and moral powers so that he may exercise these to his own greater happiness and the greater benefit of his fellow men. The major premise of this educational philosophy, as of the Christian religion and the democratic political philosophy of which it is a part, is that wisdom and virtue must be cultivated in individuals before they can be communicated to society; that man's progress as a race is governed by his progress as an individual. Centuries of experience confirm the rightness of this premise. The very origins of the industrial revolution, in individual scientific discoveries, attest to it, as do all the great works of art, music, literature, philosophy, and religion, the hallmarks of what we please to call western civilization. Could *Hamlet* have been written by a committee, or the "Mona Lisa" painted by a club? Could the New Testament have been composed as a conference report? Creative ideas do not spring from groups. They spring from individuals. The divine spark leaps from the finger of God to the finger of Adam, whether it takes ultimate shape in a law of physics or a law of the land, a poem or a policy, a sonata or a mechanical computer. Groups may exploit, change, in some cases even improve upon this creative essence; without it they would have nothing to do.

But if the individual's exercise of his creative powers is to be systematically curtailed, we may ask ourselves, why bother to cultivate them in the first place? If his success and happiness is to depend upon organizational procedures and techniques, why not substitute these for the contemplation of the good, the beautiful, and the true? This is a conclusion to which numbers of educational institutions appear to have come and toward which the tide sets strongly throughout our schools and colleges. Shall we float with it or resist it?

I hope we shall resist it, for it can be resisted. Our universities can resist it by offering their students a true liberal education. The recipients of such education can resist it by continuing to prove their extraordinary competence and versatility in the very circumstances that incline others in the opposite educational direction. Not least conspicuous in this respect is the record of those graduates in the armed forces and their prominence in the arts and in public affairs.

This is not the first time in our history that forms of organization have given pause to the champions of individual freedom, nor is it likely to be the last. Surely the creation of a national government presented our ancestors with no less formidable a problem of organization than the one with which we have to contend today. They were passionately dedicated to individual liberty. At the same time they realized that so vast and diversified a country could not hope to govern itself by a congeries of Greek city states or New England town meetings, to say nothing of the romantic notions of Rousseau. Their major premise was the freedom of the individual. Their minor premise was the need for organization. Their conclusion was the Constitution and the Bill of Rights. They accepted the need of organization and devised a form appropriate to the need. They then infused that form with respect and protection for individual freedom and initiative.

This is exactly what we must do in our time and circumstances, and the fact that it could have been done so effectively nearly two centuries ago should give us courage to believe we *can* do it. We can do it, as we can do most things, once we clearly define the problem and address ourselves to its solution with whole minds and hearts. We have heard much talk of political subversion of our form of government of recent date. I cannot but feel that it stands in greater danger of cultural submersion—that the tide of organization in our private life may engulf the last surviving instinct to preserve the safeguards of individual freedom in our public life. How we can make all this organization serve us instead of our serving it: that is our problem.

We might as well accept it as a fact that our present mode of living, with its intricate technical aspects, requires a correspondingly intricate nexus of organization. It would be foolish to talk of turning this clock back or of slowing its pendulum to the tempo of Walden Pond. It is equally foolish to consider this organization exempt from the same fundamental principles of individual freedom as are written into the Constitution. Corporations and labor unions have conferred great benefits upon their employees and members as well as upon the general public. But if power becomes too concentrated in a corporation or a union and its members are coerced into submission, or if either assumes and selfishly exploits a monopolistic position regardless of the public interest, the public safeguards of individual freedom are weakened by analogy, often by direct influence. Tyranny is tyranny, no matter who practices it; corruption is corruption. If citizens get used to these things and condone them in their private affairs, they school themselves to accept and condone them in their public affairs.

But it is not so much these more flagrant (and less frequent) transgressions as it is the everyday organizational way of life that threatens individual freedom. For the obvious transgressions there are obvious remedies at law. But what shall we say about the endless, sterile, stultifying conferences held in substitution, or in the desperate hope of substitution, for individual inventiveness; the public opinion polls whose vogue threatens even our moral and aesthetic values with the pernicious doctrine that the customer is always right; the unctuous public relations counsels that rob us of both our courage and our convictions? This continuous, daily deferral of opinion and judgment to someone else becomes a habit. The undeveloped negative remains a negative. It conjures a nightmare picture of a whole nation of yes-men, of hitch-hikers, eavesdroppers, and peeping toms, tip-toeing backward offstage with their fingers to their lips—this, the nation whose prophets once cried "Trust Thyself!"

We profess dismay at the number of our acquaintances swallowing tranquilizers and rushing off to psychiatrists to help them make up their minds. These are symptoms of a loss of self-respect by people who cannot respect what they do not know. They do not know themselves because they

177

spend so much of their time listening to somebody else. "I desire so to conduct the affairs of this administration," said Lincoln, "that if at the end, when I come to lay down the reins of power, I have lost every other friend on earth, I shall at least have one friend left, and that friend shall be deep down inside of me." It is because so many of us have not discovered this friend that we go looking for others and turn to sedatives or psychiatry for consolation when we fail to find them. This is part of the price excessive organization has exacted from us.

We can ill afford to pay it. A people that loses its self-respect is easily demoralized. Amongst such a people everything is for sale, including themselves. Art, science, politics all suffer from the basic lack of individual integrity. Here is reason enough for you gentlemen to keep the faith with your university and its philosophy of education. The welfare of your country depends upon it. Its cultural progress depends upon it. Its military security depends upon it, as tomorrow's technology is the fruit of today's scientific discovery. The creative power of the individual is more sorely needed today than ever before. This alone can save us from collective sterility. This alone can supply the great factory of America with designs worth producing.

Nor shall we recover our self-respect by chasing after it in crowds. Self-respect cannot be hunted. It cannot be purchased. It is never for sale. It cannot be fabricated out of public relations. It comes to us when we are alone, in quiet moments, in quiet places, when we suddenly realize that, knowing the good, we have done it; knowing the beautiful, we have served it; knowing the truth, we have spoken it.

The society in which we now live is not as free as the one which produced the principles according to which that society is governed. Bit by bit we have exchanged our freedom—voluntarily, for the most part, involuntarily to some

178

extent—for security, for productive efficiency, for creature comforts. But far from discounting the value of those educational principles, this puts them at a premium. Again and again in all kinds of occupations individuals educated in accordance with those principles continue to prove their effectiveness in our society, even in the innermost sanctums and strongholds of organization. Civilization can lose just so much of its freedom without losing all of it. The presence of individuals educated in these principles, who cleave to them and live according to them, is sorely needed to prevent such a catastrophe, to hold the balance between freedom and organization, to ensure the continuity of the creative process without which organization is futile.

The moral, then, is plain. To do good we must first know good; to serve beauty we must first know beauty; to speak the truth we must first know the truth. We must know these things ourselves, be able to recognize them by ourselves, be able to describe, explain, and communicate them by ourselves, and wish to do so, when no one else is present to prompt us or bargain with us. Such knowledge is the purpose of a liberal education. We must hold true to that purpose. No price, no mess of pottage, can equal its value to our country and ourselves, its citizens.

An Interview

A few years ago, Mr. Griswold, you said in an address at Johns Hopkins University that the American people once had a "sense of purpose" concerning higher education, and I believe you gave evidence of that sense of purpose by listing a number of milestones in the history of higher education in this country—the General Education Act of 1647; the founding of nine colleges before the country had even achieved political independence; the Land Ordinance of 1785; the Morrill Act, passed in the midst of the Civil War, which was so important in the establishment of state universities. Why do you think we have lost this sense of purpose? What happened to that original, clear vision of the importance of higher education?

GRISWOLD: I don't think we've ever lost our sense of purpose in education in the sense of its having been extinguished. But it has certainly been overshadowed and even eclipsed at times. The extremely rapid physical growth of the country, the enormous increase in our population, the importation of values from virtually every stratum of society and from every culture in the world—these are some of the things that have tended to confuse and weaken our sense of purpose about higher education.

It was a tidier, smaller world when that sense of purpose was first expressed in this country.

GRISWOLD: Yes, it was.

180

What were, or are, the essential ingredients of that sense of purpose?

GRISWOLD: It was a belief, an integral part of our political philosophy. The Founders of the Republic believed that to have a democracy, a self-governing republic whose power and influence would be diffused through all the people, you had to have a similar diffusion of education. Now, that is one of the ingredients of that sense of purpose: education had to play a very practical role—to make possible the functioning of a self-governing democracy. But if you will examine the writings of Jefferson and John Adams—to take two representative minds of that era—you will find that the purpose also included a truly sophisticated appreciation of aesthetic, moral, and ethical values, all of which, when combined, come very close to the purpose and to the sense of purpose that exist in the minds of educational philosophers, teachers, and administrators today. However, I'm not sure that they represent the majority today.

That original purpose, then, would be a twofold one, I take it. It would be an awareness and a conviction that there is an indispensable relationship between education and the political needs of a self-governing democracy.

GRISWOLD: Right.

And it would also include a conviction about the importance of learning for its own sake, for the enlargement of the intellect, as I believe Newman put it.

GRISWOLD: Exactly.

To the extent that this awareness or sense of purpose about education has been lost or dulled, would you say that, in part, this has flowed from the pressures exerted on a uni-

versity to pursue other than educational or intellectual ends?

GRISWOLD: As American society grew in diversity and size and in the variety of its enterprises, it put an ever increasing demand upon all educational institutions to become service institutions, so that that part of the original purpose which was practical in conception began to dominate the whole, and the majority of people who talk about education today talk about that aspect of it. Those who add to that the recognition of liberal education as a preparation for life, as a way of improving your mind and your soul, making a better individual out of yourself, are in the minority.

Sometimes I have a feeling that the people who have not been able to resist some of these service-institution pressures would like to resist them, but perhaps they are in a disadvantageous situation. Would you distinguish here between higher educational institutions that are tax-supported—and therefore perhaps more sensitive to the demands of state legislatures and other public pressures—and educational institutions that are private?

GRISWOLD: Some private institutions are just as sensitive and responsive to the uncritical demands of society as tax-supported institutions. But, of course, of all the educational institutions on the university level, the ones that are freest to determine their own policy in the face of these pressures from society are those private institutions which, in addition to being private, preserve and believe in the original purpose we have been talking about.

By including the practical-political effects of education in your definition of our sense of purpose, are you saying that the university never can be wholly dissociated from the society in which it exists?

GRISWOLD: That's right. Education in every age has been sensitive, to a degree, to the demands of society. In every generation, education has to find patrons and identify itself somehow or other with the interests of those patrons or, vice versa, bring the interests of the patrons into line with its own.

In the Middle Ages, the patron of learning was the church. Somewhat later, its patrons were the court, the nobility, and aristocratic families. In England, particularly, the aristocracy made large grants and gifts of land and endowment to the colleges of Oxford and Cambridge. Then the government stepped in as the chief patron in European education, first on the continent and then, especially during the past three decades, in Britain. In the United States, the first patron was the Congregational Church in New England, backed up by the colonial legislatures. These were gradually superseded by the alumni of the colleges, acting on impulses of gratitude and loyalty. In the nineteenth century, there developed a twofold support of American higher education—government and private philanthropy. The Morrill Act of 1862 established the land grant colleges, carrying forward the principle already established by the Land Ordinance of 1785, which provided that in every township land would be set aside for schools. And the two, government support and private philanthropy, marched along side by side. In our own century, of course, we have seen the establishment of great foundations from private fortunes—Carnegie, Rockefeller, Ford—which have come to the support of both private and public institutions of higher learning; we have seen a growing trend in individual, private support of colleges and universities by their alumni; and at the same time we have seen a tremendous rise in public support.

Then the schools have always had to rely on patronage and support from sources outside the academic community.

GRISWOLD: Yes. Education has never paid for itself anywhere in the world.

Wherever you have to look for money or support, then, there is the accompanying danger that you may end up accommodating yourself to the desires or needs of the patron.

GRISWOLD: Exactly. This is a lesson that each institution has to teach its patrons—that the university cannot compromise its principles and must not be asked or pressed to do so. The normal instinct we all have is to expect services rendered for value received, to assume that he who pays the piper calls the tune. From here it is an easy step to the sales doctrine that the customer is always right. In education the customer isn't always right. Some get honors, others pass, and others flunk.

Would you say that education of the patrons is one way to keep this problem manageable?

GRISWOLD: In addition to its responsibility for educating its students in the formal content of its curriculum, each institution—whether public or private—has a corresponding responsibility, and a very heavy one, to educate its patrons in the purposes of the institution. The reason some institutions have forged ahead of others is that they have been more enterprising and more successful in this mission.

Whose function is this educational mission to the patrons? I suppose it's the whole university's responsibility, but primarily the president's.

GRISWOLD: Everything comes down ultimately onto the shoulders of the president of the university. He must do it; but he can't do it alone. It is one of his major responsibilities; at times it becomes his principal responsibility. In fact, I sometimes feel that we who hold this office spend so much time justifying what we're doing that we don't have time to do what we're justifying. But it is the responsibility first and foremost of the president and the governing board of the university, the trustees, regents, or whatever they are called. They are, or at any rate ought to be, the principal means whereby the purposes of the university are transmitted to and explained to the laity. Then, of course, the responsibility diffuses itself throughout the institution. The faculty must be aware of this responsibility; they should treat the laity not as Philistines but as students and lay colleagues. In other words, to preserve from one generation to another the original purpose of higher education in its noblest sense, each institution must make a deliberate effort; and this must be an educational effort, not a mere invocation of tradition or display of symbols.

It has been remarked that behind every deplorable aspect in a modern university lies some public pressure that has been the cause of it.

GRISWOLD: Universities are not ivory towers; they're not abstracted out of the mainstream of American life, any more than they are abstracted out of the mainstream of English, French, German, or Russian life. They're a part of that life, and yet they are a very special part of it, with a very definite and definable set of objectives. It's up to each of the universities to communicate the sense of those purposes as widely and as significantly as possible.

In other words, while being a part of this mainstream of American life, the universities must still maintain their unique independence of function and purpose. I suppose that this in itself is one of the main needs of American life so far as higher education is concerned.

GRISWOLD: It certainly is. In the first place, teachers in universities are just as professional as the doctor is in medicine or the master painter in art. We don't heckle the surgeon as he's about to operate and tell him how to do it. We wouldn't heckle Picasso while he's working at his easel and tell him what colors to use. The educational process may not seem as recondite to the layman's eye as a surgeon's operation or an artist's painting, but it demands the same kind of professional dedication and competence; conversely, it demands of its critics a high degree of knowledge, understanding, and responsibility. The better educated a parent is, the more sophisticated is his understanding of the educational process in which his children are involved. But as that process progresses, even the most sophisticated parent must trust more and more the judgment of professional educators, just as he has to trust the judgment of his doctor or of the artist whose work he buys.

In the second place, a university must have institutional independence in order to perform the functions society expects of it—the discovery of new knowledge, the search for truth, and the development of newer and higher criteria for measuring the human performance. If one just looks askance at the press, editors are after him hammer and tongs with editorials about freedom of the press. Freedom is just as essential to the universities and to the whole process of education as it is to the press. This is a lesson the American public has yet to master. Academic freedom is just as essential to a free country as is freedom of the press, freedom of religion, or freedom of speech and assembly. It is part and parcel of these things. The university does not ask such freedom for selfish, occult, or capricious reasons. It asks it because it cannot make good its obligations to society without it. The doctor cannot help the patient who insists on making his own diagnosis; the philosopher cannot communicate his wisdom to the kibitzer who keeps telling him what to think.

I suppose one argument the layman might throw at the universities at this point—and it's the same argument used at times against the editors and publishers in this country—is this: "Who will criticize the university?" I wonder what your answer would be to that. If the university is allowed complete freedom to do as it wishes—with its money, its students, and its teachers and curriculum—who is going to provide the assurances that the university is using this freedom wisely?

GRISWOLD: The answer to the question, "Who will criticize the university?" is that, in fact, just about everybody will—and does. If there is one thing a university does not lack it is critics. It is freely and continuously criticized by individuals in every walk of life; by educational foundations and government agencies and committees; by professional societies and organizations representing the various fields in which it offers instruction; by the press, the clergy, and its own alumni; by virtually every element and agency in our society. Academic freedom by no means implies exemption from criticism. On the contrary, the whole atmosphere of a university is charged with criticism. Universities are steeped in criticism; they live by the critical process. The question is not whether this criticism will be made and the university exposed to it. The criticism is made and the university is thoroughly exposed to it. The question is which among its critics are the wisest and most penetrating; and the answer is, those whose criticism is based on relevant knowledge and truly professional qualifications. Such critics will come for the most part from the ranks of scholars, as indeed they have always come, and they must and will be heeded.

187

Perhaps we might discuss some of the specific problems of the university. One that seems to be bothering a lot of university people is the matter of specialization and vocationalism and the great proliferation of courses that seems to be involved with specialization and vocationalism. Is this a hopeless problem? Does the freshman, even at our most uncompromising Ivy League universities, already orient his educational and intellectual life for the profession or vocation he plans to enter?

GRISWOLD: I never expect to see the day when the educational process can be so many times distilled that it will be 100 per cent pure liberal education in the ideal form in which the philosophers have discussed it. Plato tells us that all ideals are laid away in Heaven; they're not expected to be achieved in this world. However, I think it is very useful to discuss ideals because if you start off discussing compromises, you're talking about two-and-a-third instead of three, or one-and-a-half instead of two: you never get the full value, the fully defined concept.

How can you educate a person for life instead of merely for a vocation?

GRISWOLD: That is a question that has occupied the wisest minds of antiquity as well as of the middle ages and the modern age. We cannot, at any rate we do not, distill out of the educational process all of the professional or vocational elements in it. This is impossible except for the one or two students you might get who could be isolated and kept thinking about nothing but ultimates. They might be so rich or so poor that they would not care about preparing for a job or a profession. But those are imaginary people. The real living student does have a vocational interest or a professional interest that tends to crystallize as he matures and progresses in his studies. Presumably more seniors know what they want to do than freshmen, so at some time between the freshman and the senior year this aim tends to develop and gather form and substance; and, as it does, it tends to influence the student in his attitude toward education and in his selection of courses. At Yale the effort is made to defer or delay the student's commitment to the vocational approach to education, or the approach that is a preparation for a profession, so as to expand to the umost his opportunity for what we call liberal education.

When you say "deferred," do you mean that a student at Yale, whatever his dawning professional or vocational aspirations might be, can be pretty well kept in the liberal arts studies for two or three years?

GRISWOLD: The tendency of Yale is to free itself more and more from the vocational demand. And it isn't just the undergraduate student who is encouraged to expand the liberal content of his studies as compared to the vocational content. In our law school, long ago, we abandoned the training of students for the bar examinations. Our law school offers, I would say, a liberal education in the law. The same is true in our medical school. The purpose of these two professional schools is not to turn out technicians; it is rather to enlarge to the utmost the students' grasp of the general meaning and significance of law and medicine. Moreover, as the record shows, this turns out in the final analysis to be the best kind of vocational training. Ever since we gave up drilling our law students for the bar examinations, their record in those examinations has improved until it is now unsurpassed, if not unequalled; and this year, against a national average of 15 per cent failure in one part of the National Board Examinations in medicine and 4 per cent in another part, there were no failures on either part among our medical students.

189

It could be argued that these results were insured by our high standards of admission; but I think they are even more directly attributable to the kind of education our law students and medical students receive after admission, and at least it proves that a liberal education in those fields did not impair their vocational aptitude.

When you have an institution such as Yale, in which the belief in this ideal of liberal education exists in reality and not just in carvings over the gateways or what is printed in the catalogues or appears in the baccalaureate address of the president, then this belief spreads through the entire institution. Its source is usually in the undergraduate curriculum and in the undergraduate college because there is where general education is offered. But then it spreads. And at Yale I think you will find respect for this ideal in all our professional schools and, of course, in our Graduate School of Arts and Sciences, where the candidates for the Ph.D. are taught. Now at the same time, to be honest about it, I've got to admit that in all of these schools—and varying according to individual predilections, body chemistry, and the like—there is some vocational attitude on the part of the students. A student may be planning to take a Ph.D. in philosophy and he may be concentrating on those courses most likely to bring him to the attention of somebody in the educational "slave market"; or he may be working to get a job in some particular institution. This is human nature and you can't purge it out of the system. But the effort to enlarge and expand liberal education is being made and with positive results.

In other words, it's the function of your university and administration and faculty to create the environment under which . . .

GRISWOLD: Let me put it this way: it is the proper function of *this* university—I don't want to preach to others—it is the proper function of this university to create and preserve that liberal environment. I think this is being true to the ideal of the university, which has come down to us and has been preserved and furthered by Yale and institutions like Yale.

What are the problems involved in maintaining this ideal tradition, this . . .

GRISWOLD: I just want to make a point here: I also think the effort to make valid the original and timeless philosophical claims of liberal education is being made by some people in many of our state universities, and that effort is growing in spite of obvious handicaps—the handicap of numbers that swamp the classrooms, the handicap of the service-station concept of the university. In spite of all that, if you look at leaders among our state universities in a perspective of, say, seventy-five years or even fifty years, you will find a very impressive growth of interest in and respect for the kind of values we've been talking about. Now you will also find a corresponding growth of the vocational kind of learning in those same institutions which gives them an . . .

An ambiguous character?

GRISWOLD: Yes. It's almost impossible to generalize about them because they embody such discrete and disparate values. But I don't mean to imply that it's only Yale and Harvard and Princeton that are doing these things.

What is involved in maintaining, and strengthening, your tradition of liberal learning at a school like Yale? These things do not perpetuate themselves, do they? How do you retain your faculty and attract consistently superior students? Or is maintenance of a tradition not particularly difficult?

GRISWOLD: Well, I happen to think that the purposes of liberal learning and liberal education are central to the purposes of all education. And from one generation to another this truth is perceived and understood by the best students, by the best minds. This makes for an almost automatic selector of both students and faculty. It means, I think, that the people who are seriously attracted to Yale and institutions like Yale have thought about these matters and are drawn here by these values. I'm sure this is true of our faculty. The environment that exists here is one of liberal education. It flourishes, for example, in the groups of our faculty that constitute the fellowships in our twelve residential colleges. There's a spirit that prevails among these fellowships which is comparable to the academy of Socrates or the literary club of Samuel Johnson. It is a remarkable thing, and these people enjoy it and benefit by it. You ask, "How do you maintain these values?" First, you've got to be able to identify them. Second, you've got to understand them. Third, you've got to believe in them.

What about the severe shortage of good teachers? A recent editorial in the New Republic *observed that the better schools among the 1,800 colleges and universities in this country get the cream of the new crop of teachers each year; a great many other potential teachers are attracted to commercial and technological industries. And the vast majority of our colleges must be satisfied with mediocre teachers.*

GRISWOLD: There is no doubt about it: in relation to the country's needs, as well as to the incidence of talent among its citizens, there is a dearth of able scholars and teachers in higher education. In a system of higher education as diversified as ours, I don't think it likely that we shall ever achieve completely uniform institutional standards in this respect, or equal division of this talent. Some institutions will always be stronger than others, and the ablest scholars and teachers will be attracted to the strongest institutions. Nevertheless, much can be done to improve the present situation . . .

GRISWOLD: Improvement in the salary scale to make the teaching profession in its highest branches more competitive with other professions; this means a larger allocation of national wealth to education—something we can easily afford.

A more efficient sorting out of candidates for higher education according to demonstrable aptitude and competence, with allocations of teachers and educational facilities appropriate to their respective needs. The whole burden cannot be borne by the graduate schools of the leading universities. The standards of these schools must not be lowered, and the value of the Ph.D. must be pegged to these standards, or the whole system will suffer from inflation. The effort should be made to bring as many graduate schools as possible up to these standards.

In addition, training programs for high school teachers who wish to move up to the college or junior college level should be introduced.

Many more college-educated and university-educated women should be recruited on both part-time and full-time bases.

There should be much greater mobility for teachers in the four critical years that form an educational continuity in the academic curriculum, namely the last two years of high school and the first two years of college.

The whole teaching profession should be made more attractive, not just in terms of money but in terms of professional duties, intellectual prospects, and human possibilities.

I myself look beyond the graduate schools of arts and sciences in the universities for the main trouble in this whole situation. I think that if the curriculum of the teacher-training programs for secondary education could be made more liberal, this would be the greatest single thing that could be done to increase the flow of competent and properly trained people throughout the whole system of education, including higher education. It's at the secondary school level that these values are most desperately corrupted. They are corrupted by a curriculum, a program of pedagogy which is a methodology of teaching that really has the effect of repelling instead of attracting the ablest teachers, those who would be most likely to influence their students to go into the teaching profession.

High school is certainly the most impressionable period in a young person's life.

GRISWOLD: Yes, and it's right here that the university loses the battle. Many times you will find that an eventual Ph.D. candidate was originally inspired by his English teacher, or his history or math or science teacher in secondary school to consider the academic profession. The educational experience is a highly personal thing, and in many instances it is one single gifted teacher who has inspired a number of students. Now we need more of that kind of teacher, and we're not going to get them out of methodological pedagogy. This has got to be cleared up so that the people who are interested in teaching and who are thinking about it as a career can see it in a clear light, so that they can perceive the liberal values in education, the values we've been discussing. There's no lack of potential teachers of great imagination and ability. But they can't find any inspiration in the fog of pedagogy.

This is something a lot of people are talking and writing about these days. Is there evidence that something remedial is being done about it?

GRISWOLD: There is evidence that some of those responsible for the kind of teacher training we call "pedagogy" are not as well satisfied with it as they professed to be twenty-five years ago. There's been much debate about this, and some self-criticism in certain quarters. I think a great deal more can be done. Of course you know as well as I do that you're up against a political problem here in that the whole teacher-training curriculum has been frozen into law in many states. There are certification requirements, and if you will examine them you will find that many are the icicles of the old system of pedagogy. And behind these laws stands a militant organization with branches in every state and elaborate headquarters in Washington. It's very hard indeed when you have a group of people defending an organization as such to get them to stop and say what the organization is for. I do not intend to give a discourse here on the teacher-training program in this country, but I believe that the solution to the problem of an adequate number of properly trained, competent teachers in the universities lies first in the change of the curriculum for the training of high school teachers. It is there that you've got to get the initial impulse transmitted from the active teacher to the potential teacher.

I suppose the shortage of teachers cannot be separated from the maximization of the number of students, and this is tied up with the idea that every American has a right, a birth-right, to a college education. Of course, Yale is not too affected, I imagine, by that national feeling, but . . .

GRISWOLD: Well, we're not unaware of it.

But I mean that this aggravates the teacher supply problem. When we talk about teacher shortages, we're also talking about the increase in the number of students, many of whom perhaps should not even be in a college classroom.

GRISWOLD: I believe we've got all the necessary talent in this country to produce a proper ratio of trained, competent teachers to the number of students. What is lacking is the sense of purpose. Inasmuch as this sense of purpose can be best communicated by people who understand the full meaning of liberal education, the aim should be to increase that kind of education to its proper, proportionate part of the whole, and we ought to begin this enterprise where it is most needed at the moment, namely in the curriculum of the high school teachers, in their teacher-training programs.

Would you care to say anything about the perennial problem of the ratio of research to teaching? Do you have any problem in this regard at Yale? We hear it said that prestige and status in the academic world seem to be shifting from the teaching of undergraduates to research work in the laboratories.

GRISWOLD: As long as there are universities, this problem will exist. I don't think it will ever be finally solved because in every case it comes down to the individual.

Is there an optimum balance between teaching and research?

GRISWOLD: Institutionally, yes, but not individually. It's very hard to find an individual in whom you can achieve an optimum balance. Nine times out of ten he's bound to be either more of a teacher than a scholar or more of a scholar than a teacher. But I think the conflict between the two is greatly exaggerated. In the sciences, for example, the familiar criticism is made that the university scientist doesn't pay as much attention to his teaching as he does to his research. But for a scientist there is less difference between teaching and research because he's got to do his teaching in the laboratory; his best teaching is done there. If you analyze this problem and ask exactly what one means by "research" and "teaching" and ask whether it is really true that Professor X doesn't teach but just "does research," or vice versa, you soon find out that even though Professor X may seem to be spending most of his time in the library or in the laboratory he has attracted students, a circle . . .

Disciples?

GRISWOLD: Yes, so he is teaching. The distinction is really between the lecturers to large classes who are particularly good at that on the one hand and, on the other hand, the scholar who is most at home—and most effective as a teacher —when actually participating in his scholarship and sharing the experience with his students. Both of these men exist in a university. It isn't easy in a university to maintain an exact optimum balance between the two because a university is a community of individuals and they make their own plans as individuals; but a reasonable institutional optimum can be achieved—although obviously in a university more of the energy of the community that makes up the university is going to be invested in research than would be true in the independent liberal arts college that emphasizes teaching.

Do you try to get as much of the talent and energy you have on the graduate level into as much teaching as possible?

GRISWOLD: I think I can say that Yale has been consistent in its efforts to maintain a high standard of undergraduate teaching, and a similarly high standard of teaching in its graduate and professional schools. Ours are small schools. The ratio of teachers to students in our professional schools is higher than it is in other schools. We try to maintain the closest possible contact between the faculty and the students. We do not subscribe to the proposition that this would be a first-rate university if only there weren't any students around. On the other hand, a considerable amount of the intellectual and physical energy of our faculty does go into research, and that is proper. From the standpoint of the student, even of the undergraduate student, if he's at all curious intellectually and not just sitting on the small of his back waiting to be entertained, he's bound to learn more from the man who is himself learning than he is from the man who just tells him about learning.

David Riesman discussed some of the attractions of the teaching profession, one of them being the satisfaction of the intellectual's desire for what Riesman called "colleagueship," the intellectual companionship of one specialist for another in his own field, but, more importantly, the companionship of specialists in the other fields represented at a great university.

GRISWOLD: I don't think many people—even Yale graduates realize the size of Yale's faculty in comparison with its student body. We have a student body of just under 8,000 all told—that is, the undergraduates combined with graduate and professional students. And we have more than 2,000 people in faculty status. These are not all full-time teachers or combination teacher-scholars. Some of them are laboratory assistants and some are research assistants. But all of them are engaged in the process of discovering knowledge, interpreting knowledge, and communicating knowledge. And there are more than 2,000 of them. Now this becomes a very expensive operation, as you can imagine. But it does produce what Riesman is talking about—a sufficiently diversified intellectual society so that the most uncompromising specialist can find at least one other like himself to talk to. It is a most cosmopolitan community, in which any scholar can find other scholars with tastes and interests congenial to his own.

How do you conceive of a university president's responsibility to the faculty? On what terms would you express this responsibility? Certainly the university president defends his faculty from outside, non-academic pressures. But in addi-

tion, do you think a university president should make a pur-poseful, continuing effort to maintain some kind of personal contact with his faculty? If so, can that be done in a school with, say, 2,000 faculty members?

GRISWOLD: A university president's responsibility is to share —and enlarge—the professional ideals and endeavors of the faculty, to work to the limit of his personal, official, and institutional resources toward that end. He must protect the faculty's independence by maintaining the independence of the university. Beyond that his responsibility to the faculty proliferates in almost endless detail. This is something each individual who holds the office has to deal with in his own way. I have been a member of the Yale faculty for thirty years and I like to see my colleagues. I enjoy their company and benefit from it.

I've heard the criticism that at large universities there is an unavoidable impersonalism and lack of contact between the president and his teachers.

GRISWOLD: So have I. The president will do everything he can to show the faculty his sympathy and friendliness as well as his devotion to his and their common cause. But the demands on his time, energy, and intellectual resources are infinite, while he is finite. He must have the wit and the judgment to distinguish between the essential and the non-essential; between the things he would like to do, he can do, he ought to do, and he must do; and he must exercise that judgment. How effective he will be in this will depend on his own character and resourcefulness; on his inner feelings for his profession and his university; on his intellectual curiosity, his capacity—and desire—for intellectual growth; and on other subtleties (and chances) that can never be reduced to system and learned out of books.

199

To come back, for a moment, to the matter of pressures on the universities. Here is one pressure that may be a legitimate one. We are told that universities should seriously re-examine their history, social science, and political science departments, and, I suppose, the anthropological areas as well, in the light of the United States' new responsibility in world affairs. Does the changing international scene place a new burden on the university so far as preparing its students is concerned?

GRISWOLD: These things have not created new burdens so much as they have added new weight and importance to old burdens. The United States has always been involved in world affairs, and the changing international scene, as you call it, has been in a state of almost continuous change since the beginning of history—just as the laws and properties of nuclear energy recently discovered by modern physics have always existed. The trouble has been that our knowledge and understanding of these facts and forces, in world affairs as in physics, have been rudimentary and inadequate. The university's job is not to solve the immediate problems and crises in world affairs as they arise—the underdeveloped nations, Berlin, Laos, Cuba, and the rest—but to bring our fundamental knowledge and understanding of the forces that produce these problems and crises—the historical, cultural, economic, and scientific trends and causes underlying them—up to date. And not so much up to date as up to scratch. The best way to accomplish this is for the universities to encourage and enable their scholars in the basic fields and disciplines—especially history, foreign languages and literature, economics, and anthropology—to press forward their studies on a truly universal plane. The only newness in this responsibility lies in projecting their respective data-gathering and interpreting techniques and procedures into heretofore neglected, non-Western areas, nations, and cultures. They must revise the intellectual map of the world to make it coincide with the physical map.

As to what all this implies for our curriculum, for the training of students, here again I think it means that we should do more faithfully and effectively things we ought to have been doing anyway, rather than that we should do a whole lot of new things. In the first place, a university's responsibility for the general diffusion of knowledge necessary to the process of self-government is no different with respect to world affairs from its responsibility with respect to national affairs; and in both respects the most sophisticated minds of every age have found the ideal training for the ideal citizen to be a good, sound liberal education. I believe this is still true provided the education is given, as it should be, universal perspective and significance, by the inclusion of universal and not merely Western data. I think it holds true, too, for the training of prospective diplomats and other experts who will devote their careers to world affairs or will be called upon to turn to them from other careers. World affairs is another name for world politics, and world politics is politics. Politics is not and never can be a science. The human race is not that logical or inert or controllable. Politics is an art, one that has been called the art of the possible. The best possible preparation for the practice of this art is, in my opinion, a good, sound liberal education given relevance to world affairs by taking the world for its province as it ought to do anyway.

I won't talk to you about the problem of attracting superior students because I think Yale gets its share of these and can be highly selective in its admissions procedure.

GRISWOLD: Well, we're in a position, fortunately, to be able to be fairly selective. We didn't come by that easily. After all, we've been at it for over 260 years; and we've had our ups and downs like everybody else.

In this matter of selectivity of students, the big state universities are somewhat disadvantaged, aren't they, because by law they must accept every applicant for admission?

GRISWOLD: Yes, but at the end of the freshman year there is a decimation of the ranks. It is then that the educational authority of the university catches up with the political authority of the community.

But meanwhile, what a waste of energy and time for the university!

GRISWOLD: A great waste. But, as I've said earlier, some of our state universities are doing a better job in sorting these people out and putting the bright ones in blue-ribbon courses than some of our private institutions may imagine.

Do you think the university, as such, bears any direct responsibility for the moral and spiritual health of our society? If so, in what way do you think the university can best discharge that responsibility? By formal courses in religion, theology, ethics? By attempting to confront students with a maximum number of teachers who are themselves living examples of morally and religiously motivated men? By insistence on the highest, most uncompromising intellectual standards of teaching, on the grounds that the moral and spiritual realities will be communicated by superior teachers who, because of their superiority, cannot and would not neglect them?

GRISWOLD: Every basic institution in society bears a direct responsibility for that society's moral health. This is particularly true in a democracy, where society is self-governing, and self-government begins with government of the self. The university bears a large and exceptionally important part of this responsibility. After all, its broad objective is a society of educated men, and I don't think we need to argue the proposition that moral values are more likely to flourish in an educated society than in an uneducated one.

As to the specific ways in which a university discharges its responsibility for our moral and spiritual welfare, there are many, including and in addition to those which you mention. What is highly significant in this respect is the ethical imperative imposed by the search for truth on all who take part in it. No one can spend much time in a university without sensing this; those who take the purposes of the university at all seriously are powerfully influenced by it themselves and communicate that influence to others. Again, the discovery of truth, especially scientific truth, brings with it spiritual revelation, even exaltation, in the perception of law and order in the universe. Moreover, the inspiration that comes with the contemplation of man's great aesthetic achievements and the study of the lives and work of great men in every field—all standard fare in a university —is both moral and spiritual as well as intellectual.

At the same time, we must remember that a university's responsibility for the moral and spiritual welfare of society, important as it is, is not exclusive. It is shared by two other institutions, namely the family and the church. If these do not make the contributions expected of them in the case of an individual student, it is unlikely that the university will be able to do the job all by itself.

As I have already pointed out, the university and the church are ancient allies in the educational process. Both recognize the subtle gradations of meaning between wisdom, truth, and virtue. I believe that in both moral and spiritual affairs and the things that connect them the experience of living in a university community is much more likely to strengthen both than it is to weaken either. I think this is shown in the conduct of life of its members. Generally speaking, a university is an idealistic community, and the best ones provide models of what the civilized world should provide for us all.

Do you think the university should reflect in its faculty and curriculum the religious and moral pluralism characteristic of the American society at large? Is this the responsibility of each university, or of all the universities combined? Do you think each individual university should or can reflect this religious and moral pluralism on its campus, or is it sufficient that the universities in the aggregate should reflect this pluralism?

GRISWOLD: Universities such as Yale, originally Protestant but now independent and non-denominational, preserve their original Protestant character and at the same time encourage religious pluralism. Thus, at Yale we have a university church that is Congregational in character, and a university chaplain who is a Presbyterian. At the same time, we give hospitality to the chaplains and communicants of many other denominations and faiths, including both Catholic and Jewish as well as Protestant. I think that this is a good thing for Yale, for Protestantism, and, to the extent that Yale may serve as a model community, a good thing for the country. At the same time, there are denominational institutions which place much greater emphasis on their own faiths. Both types of institutions have a right to do as they wish in these matters and both contribute, each in a different way, to the religious pluralism of the country. Personally, I believe that religion is a private affair, for institutions as well as people, and the main thing is to respect one another's privacy.

Someone, I think Dr. Hutchins, has said that while it is not necessary that all the professors on a university's faculty be religious men, it is desirable that all of them at least "take religion seriously." Do you agree with that assertion?

GRISWOLD: Yes, I agree entirely.

Do you think it is true, as we have been hearing in recent years, that the moral and spiritual life of America has been declining? If so, what do you think the university can do, if anything, to help halt the decline and reverse the trend?

GRISWOLD: At times I think our moral and spiritual life is declining: at times I do not think so; and I suspect that at both times the facts correspond with and substantiate my impressions and observations. The current runs both ways, and it would take a major prophet to determine which is the stronger. But surely we aren't doing as well as we could be doing in these respects, or as well as we should be doing. I have already suggested various ways in which the university may contribute, but I should like to repeat that the university cannot be expected to do the job alone, without the support of the family and the church. In my own opinion, there is much slack to be taken up by both of these. The family has become too scared of its children; the children too insecure in their remoteness from their parents; and the church too much of a social welfare organization for the good of the family or the church or society. Although I believe that everything I have said about a university's responsibility for our moral and spiritual welfare is true, it could discharge this responsibility to its own students more immediately, more readily, and more fruitfully if their homes had got them more actively concerned with moral values and their churches with spiritual values.

Do you think there has been, say in the last generation, an increase of intellectual skepticism and relativism? If so, would this in itself tend to persuade university students that the "smart" and "sophisticated" person is the one who is skeptical and relativistic about his moral and spiritual life as well?

GRISWOLD: There has no doubt been a trend in this direction among undergraduates. But I believe it is a superficial one supported more by the alternating bravado and self-conscious conformism characteristic of the age group than by deep-seated conviction or belief. Underneath, in his true self, I believe that the modern undergraduate has just as sound ethical instincts and just as great a capacity for spiritual growth as his parents; that he affects an attitude of fatalism in the face of impersonal forces which threaten his premature extinction; and that he is, in reality, struggling upward from the depths for a breath of air and something solid to hang onto.

In general, do you believe that the university, through its traditional truth-seeking and critical function has, as a matter of history, done an excellent, good, or fair job in producing graduates who have contributed to the positive formation of the American character?

GRISWOLD: I believe that in general, in these terms, some universities have done an excellent job, others a good job, others a fair job, all together an essential job which is capable of improvement.

THE YALE PAPERBOUNDS